ISBN number and
code goes here

# Lead Like Mary

Barry Dore

# Praise for 'Lead Like Mary'

All the wisdom but none of the cheesiness normally associated with this topic.

Barry shares his comprehensive understanding of the key traits of great leaders with refreshing honesty and in an engaging personal way.

This is a book about a complex topic which is accessible, to the point and easy to read. It feels like Barry is talking to you, not writing, and certainly not lecturing.

This book is an easy read, but the implications for all of us are far from easy. This is not about him it is about us/you. If you have never read a book about the key components of leadership before, start here.

It is relevant to all of us. Whether you are just setting out on your career or have already progressed a long way into it I'd recommend reading this and using it to examine yourself honestly. It takes courage to do this and to address what you see, but this is one of Barry's key points, without courage none of us will change ourselves or the world for the better.

This concise but comprehensive short book captures the essence of other great thinkers and points us in their direction should we want to read more. But if we all followed the mantras in this book there is little doubt we would be far far more effective as individuals, as organisations and as a society. Barry brings his own wisdom and makes theory real.

All too often genuine wise words on leadership are undermined by the messenger's style. But in this book Barry uses straight forward language with no jargon and in his English way based on real experience he talks about the key components of true leadership

*Stephanie Hilborne OBE*
*Chief Executive, The Wildlife Trusts*


Over the past 5 years Barry has supported our journey to build effective leadership and a high performance culture across our marketing teams. Many of the tools he has shared with us have become part of our common language, enabling powerful, honest communication and building trust between colleagues. Within this time, I have seen many individuals who he has worked with grow considerably as people and as leaders.

Using Barry's conversational and common sense approach, this book brings together a set of effective principles and practical tools that can help us all become better leaders. It's easy to read and I found the self reflection questions at the end of each chapter highly valuable in challenging and inspiring my leadership journey.

Whether it's "having the right people on the bus" or giving "freedom within a framework", I'm sure that I will continually return to this book as a valuable reminder of actions and behaviours that will get the best from our people and so drive outstanding results for our businesses.

*Linda Doughty*
*Group Marketing Services Director, Travis Perkins plc*


A truly inspiring read. Leaders at every level can learn a great deal from Mary.

*Tim Mackrill*
*Osprey Project, Rutland Water*

Leadership can help you advance on all levels and in all aspects of your life. Leadership begins with yourself. The powerful message of this stimulating and accessible book challenges the idea that leadership is something somehow reserved for bosses and CEOs, showing instead that you can lead at all levels in an organisation, community or family.

Its inspiring, practical reflections will equip you with the passion to improve and persist. If you see yourself as a leader this book could help you unlock your potential and make a positive difference to your life and to those around you.

*Rachel Colley*
*Project Officer, University of the West of England*

I have known Barry for over 35 years. We started our leadership journeys together as elected student officers. I still refer back to a number of the lessons I learned back then as a well-meaning, but callow youth. Mainly lessons learned from the things I did wrong! All these years later, after an executive career that included 15 years on the Board of Tesco plc, I agree with Barry when he says we still have so much to learn about effective leadership.

I enjoyed Barry's book. It is full of wisdom, but is approachable and easy to grasp. To do anything well requires thought, application and experience. Leadership is no different.

Businesses require leaders throughout the organisation, and as Barry brings out, we have all worked with, and for plenty of people who lead badly! Lead Like Mary should make a useful contribution to trying to correct that all-too-common problem.

*Andrew Higginson*
*Ex Finance & Strategy Director, Tesco plc (ex Entertainments Officer, Birmingham Polytechnic Students' Union)*

In the modern manufacturing environment there is a continuous improvement mantra associated with procedures and processes. Sadly, the continuous improvement of leaders is not so well embraced. In 'Lead Like Mary' Barry has shared the observations and tools that he utilised to help guide me during my journey to becoming a better leader.

*David Bernard*
*Director of Global Operations, Cytec*

Barry is an evangelist of truly great leadership, his coaching and leadership material have not only helped transform my working career, but also what I have learnt continues to inspire me to strive to be a better leader than I was yesterday

*Hannah Apps*
*Senior Usability Manager, Travis Perkins plc*

# Acknowledgements

To Jakkie, for inspiring me to write about Mary, for believing in me, and challenging my own beliefs

To Katherine and her team at Brand Magic for their help, support and patience, and to Victoria, for her painstaking proof reading

To the many people who generously gave their time to read the drafts and offered such sage and practical advice, especially Rachel and Linda.

To the 'Marys', and those striving to be Mary, that I have the privilege to work with, and who inspire me every day

'Come on the amazing journey and learn all you should know'

The Who, 1969

# Foreword

By Lesley Dixon,
Chief Executive, PSS

I was delighted when Barry asked me to write the foreword for this book. It has all the characteristics I like best in books on leadership - it is written in an easy to read style; it has plenty of ideas you can implement and - well - it just makes sense.

Barry's own experience puts him in an ideal position to be able to write this book. His views on leadership have been formed over many years and through many different experiences. Whether that's learning on the job having been thrown in at the deep end as a young leader; learning from others in a large corporate (both how to and how not to lead!); learning from watching and supporting many people over the years as a coach or developing his own thoughts though self development.

This book puts together some of the best thinking in modern leadership. To get the most out of some of the ideas then further reading would help (this is well signposted) but this is a great place to start. And for those of you already familiar with some of the books referenced, well it's a reminder of those lessons that day to day we can too easily forget.

So why do I think this book makes sense? The one word that sums up this book for me is easy. It's easier to work with the right people; it's easier to work with people who are effective; it's easier to work with people who are motivated by what they do; it's easier to work with people who know what's expected of them and are bought into it; it's easier (and makes for a more enjoyable working life!) to show an interest in people; and it's easier to work with people who are working to their maximum potential. And whilst dealing with any kind of poor performance isn't easy, it's easier to deal with it early on rather than wait until it becomes a major issue further down the line. And it's not hard to bring those things about. Yes it takes resilience; it also takes time. But to do the opposite is very hard indeed! And this book explains why this approach works and how you can lead in a way that will make it happen.

At PSS we are trying to create something very special. Our history is special – we were there at the beginning of Age Concern, Citizens Advice Bureau and Legal Aid to name but three. But resting on our laurels is not something we want to do. And we know that to create that something special, well, we will only do this through our people.

We don't want an organisation of 'Bills' or 'Sidneys'; we want an organisation full of 'Marys'. And by having our values at the heart of what we do and practicing so many of the ideas contained in this book then we are on our way to making that happen. I don't claim to behave like Mary 100% of the time, but I try to do so, because for me, there is no other way.

So my advice is read this book, think about the ideas therein and then make a point of doing those easy, common sense, "why wouldn't you" things and make everyone's lives (including your own) a whole heap better. Put simply, lead like Mary and, in time, you can create a team or even an organisation that is capable of doing anything that it wants!

*Lesley Dixon is Chief Executive of UK social enterprise PSS. She joined the organisation in 2009 and has since made a huge impact on the structure, shape and direction of the organisation.*

*PSS is a social enterprise that works across the UK helping people get the most from life, whether this is at home, in their families, in their health and well-being or within their wider support networks.*

*As an organisation PSS developed some of the best known names in community support including Age Concern, the Citizen's Advice Bureau and Legal Aid and in 2019 will celebrate its 100th birthday. Today the team sits alongside Local Government and NHS services plugging the gaps and providing 'on the ground' support for a wide array of people.*

*Over the past four years Lesley has reshaped PSS, forming a structure that is ready to return to its roots, enabling it to once again lead the way in improving lives across the UK.*

*Today social care is incredibly topical through concerns about current cuts, future capacity and Governmental commitment to the sector. By having innovation at its heart and Lesley at its helm, I have no doubts PSS will put Liverpool back on the map as the birthplace of creative thinking that changes lives.*

Barry Dore

# Contents

Chapter ONE      An Amazing Journey      2

Chapter TWO      Bill and Sidney      14

Chapter THREE      Meet Mary      24

Chapter FOUR      Serving Others      34

Chapter FIVE      Personally Effective      46

Chapter SIX      Values-Led and Courageous      64

Chapter SEVEN      Trusting and Trustworthy      80

Chapter EIGHT      Right People on the Bus      96

Chapter NINE      A Visionary who Executes      112

Chapter TEN      Absolute Clarity      124

Chapter ELEVEN      Freedom Within a Framework      138

Chapter TWELVE      Joint Accountability      154

Chapter THIRTEEN      Relentlessness      166

Chapter FOURTEEN      Becoming Mary      178

So now what?      184

# Chapter ONE
## An Amazing Journey

'Leadership is not something that you learn once and for all. It is an ever-evolving pattern of skills, talents and ideas that grow and change as you do.'

Sheila Bethel

'The times they are a-changin'

Bob Dylan

Leadership is my passion. Through a working career spanning almost forty years I have tried to understand what makes a truly effective leader. I have thought back to my own leadership style and experiences, over a career in large companies and smaller organisations. I have reflected on the strengths and weaknesses of the many leaders I worked for and with, both good, and too often bad. Since setting up my own business several years ago, I have had the opportunity to study the effectiveness of the many leaders I work with, some inspirational, many striving to do the right thing, and some, quite frankly, shocking.

As a young man in my twenties, I set out on my leadership journey as the general manager of a small charity. This was a baptism of fire. As boss of the organisation at a very young age, I was inexperienced with few people to guide me. I blundered through by trial and error, often making it up as I went along.

Through my thirties and into my forties I worked for fifteen years for a major brewing and leisure company. Here, I had a career path set out for me, rising over the years from Territory Sales Manager to Regional Managing Director.

I was sent on numerous management training programmes. I learned about strategy, climbed mountains and built rafts. I worked for some appalling leaders, many mediocre ones and very occasionally an inspirational one. I learned a lot, too often about how not to lead.

All around me I saw great people with so much potential still untapped inside them. I saw people who had so much to give but were held back by poor leadership, lack of clarity, little support, limited freedom, low trust and suffocating processes. I just knew it could be so different, that there was a much better way of leading.

Then, as often happens in such large companies, an exit opportunity appeared. The company sold 1,000 of its units, and a senior team, including me, went with the sale. Suddenly, we had the opportunity to do things differently, to create a new culture, to build trust, to give freedom with accountability, to lead in a very different way. It was an exhilarating journey, which was over in two years when we sold the business on. I will tell more of that story later.

These experiences convinced me that the time was right to do something by myself. To set up my own business working with people at every level, to challenge them to lead in a way that unlocked the potential of their people.

I was convinced that once this was done, anything was possible.

The last dozen years have been hard work, often frustrating, but above all a joy. I have worked with some amazing people across all types of organisations, large and small, in private, public and voluntary sectors. I have focussed on helping to unlock potential, develop leadership capability and build effectiveness - of people, teams and organisations. I have read widely and studied leadership and taken part in countless discussions on what makes a great leader.

Here's the thing. After almost forty years of experiencing, observing and studying leadership, I feel I still know so little. It is such an enormous and complex subject! Search on-line and you will find literally millions of leadership references. As Sheila Bethel said in the above quote, you never stop learning about leadership. The journey never ends.

What has emerged from my countless experiences and observations, is an absolute conviction that how people lead at every level, has such an impact on those around them and on the effectiveness of whole organisations. Great leaders can unlock potential everywhere; they can transform lives, make a truly amazing difference and deliver amazing, sustainable results.

Conversely, poor leaders can create havoc, block progress, leave potential untapped - even destroy organisations. These poor leaders come in all shapes and sizes, from egotistical bullies to weak, indecisive leaders, unable to take decisions.

This may paint a depressing, if all too familiar, picture. From the midst of it all however, I sense a change is happening. I increasingly see examples of a new generation of leaders emerging that want things to be different. I work with these emerging leaders every day. They can be found in all shapes and sizes of organisations across the private, public and voluntary sectors. Some are at the top of their organisations, but many others are nearer to the beginning of their leadership journey, in more junior roles, just starting to build their careers.

What unites these many leaders, is their desire and commitment to lead in the right way. They want to build successful teams and organisations, they want to deliver great results, but they want to ensure they do things right. They care about people. They care about the world around them. They want to make a difference. Their leadership philosophy is based on serving others, on unlocking potential. They have deep rooted beliefs and values that determine what they do.

Many others with far greater minds than me, including Stephen Covey, Ken Blanchard, Jim Collins and John Kotter have explored this philosophy over the years and I share some of their thinking in this book.

There is no revolution happening here - but I do sense evolution taking place. Things are changing and **you** could be part of it.

The one certainty that has emerged from my years of observation and study, is there is no one model or style for a perfect leader. I do believe there are a set of universal and timeless principles which underpin leadership:

## Anyone can be a leader. It's a choice

Sometimes, when we think of leaders we think of those people at the top of organisations, Chief Executives and Directors, but anyone can be a leader - it is a choice we make. Leaders can exist at every level within the organisational hierarchy. We do not even need to line manage another person in order to be a leader. Leaders exist everywhere, including the front line, where they lead through their influence and personal credibility.

## Leadership is a whole life activity

Leadership is not something we just do in our professional lives. Every one of us can lead outside work as well - in our roles as parents, relatives, friends, in voluntary activities, in communities. Leadership replicates through every aspect of life.

## Leadership is an inside-out activity

The principle of inside-out leadership has been explored by many, including Stephen Covey and Kevin Cashman. As illustrated in the 'inside out leadership' model, we can, and do lead at three levels - in all three circles. Leadership can and must only start in the inner circle. This is where we lead ourselves, the beginning of the leadership journey. When we are leading ourselves effectively we are taking control of ourselves, making choices, building our personal effectiveness and modelling the behaviours we want to see in others.

Only when we lead ourselves effectively, do we gain the ability and legitimacy to lead in the middle circle. This circle consists of all those people immediately around us. These are people who, metaphorically, we touch daily. At work this will include our team, our colleagues, our boss, and those real people in other organisations with whom we have regular contact.

Outside work, our family and friends are in this circle, together with people in our leisure pursuits and those in our local community. If we choose to, we can play a leadership role with all of these people - helping, enabling, guiding and teaching them. Our right and ability to do so comes from our strength in the inner circle.

It is through our effectiveness in the middle circle that we gain the opportunity to begin to make a difference in the outer circle. Out there is everything else.

Our whole organisation and beyond, our wider neighbourhood, governments, society - ultimately the whole world. Every single one of us could make an impact in this circle, but only ever from the inside out.

# Inside Out Leadership

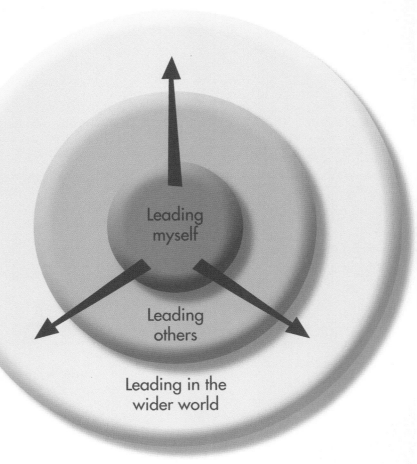

Leading
myself

Leading
others

Leading in the
wider world

## Leadership is based on a series of timeless principles

Truly effective leadership is not demonstrated through techniques and quick fixes. It lies deep within us, it is character based. It is 'values-led' and rooted in timeless principles of effectiveness. When we lead from the 'inside-out' we lead with genuineness and integrity. It's our route to becoming an authentic leader.

## Leaders can be born, but they also can be made

People often describe great leaders as being born, not made. I am convinced both are possible. Of course, some people are born leaders, but many others can develop the skills, attributes, self-awareness, understanding and experience to become effective leaders throughout their lives.

## Leaders can change the world

Great leaders can deliver transformational change. They can improve lives, unlock potential, deliver lasting solutions - whatever the world they are working in or contributing to. As Margaret Mead said:

> 'never doubt that a small group of thoughtful, committed citizens can change the world. Indeed, it's the only thing that ever has'

So, whilst I believe many different leadership styles can exist and there is no one single model for effective leadership, my many years of working with and observing countless leaders, has convinced me that there are a common set of traits that define great leaders. I believe that the leaders I see who demonstrate, or aspire to demonstrate these common traits, are at the forefront and heart of the leadership evolution I see emerging around me.

As I have identified and observed these traits, I have developed a fictional leadership character I have called Mary, in order to better articulate them. Mary is not based entirely on one leader, but instead has grown from a whole series of real people I have worked with, as traits have emerged.

Exploring leadership, becoming a great leader, truly making a difference to the world around you, is an amazing journey. As Sheila Bethel said:

'Leadership is an ever-evolving pattern of skills, talents and ideas that grow and change as you do.'

By leading from the inside-out and by focussing on developing the traits we explore in this book, you too can become an even more highly effective leader, making a real difference to those around you. It doesn't matter whether you are Chief Executive of a large company, an accountant, an IT or marketing manager, a sales assistant, a nurse or health care worker, or helping run a community association or scout group - the principles are the same. It's about who you are, not what you are.

In this book I invite you to meet Mary, to examine her traits with me, and then to embark on your own amazing leadership journey. It's a book that has taken a year to write, but has been forty years in the making.

But first let's meet Bill and Sidney

# Notes

12

# Chapter TWO
## Bill and Sidney

'Leadership is an opportunity to serve.
It is not a trumpet call to self-importance'

J Donald Walters

'The measure of a man is what he does with power'

Pittacus

I was facilitating a leadership programme recently and we were talking about the kind of boss who is highly autocratic, even a bully. I noticed one of the group becoming quite animated. 'I know someone just like that', she said, 'my brother works for him!'

She went on to discuss, passionately and emotionally, her brother's experiences. He works as a store manager for a major UK retailer. His boss is the Regional Director, running maybe twenty stores. She described this boss as horrendous to work for - a complete bully. He made his people's lives a misery, constantly berating and undermining them in front of colleagues. Nobody escaped his intimidating wrath. Ringing his managers at all times of day and night, making completely unreasonable demands on sales performance and cost cutting. He seemed to take great pleasure from the anguish he caused his people, publicly humiliating them.

We asked this person why her brother continued to do the job. 'He's found it impossible to find another role', she confided, 'he has tried, but as soon as a recruitment agency or prospective employer learns where he works now, they are not interested. This company has a reputation in the industry for this kind of behaviour. They just treat their people like dirt.'

Powerful stuff - but unfortunately all too common. Let me introduce Bill, an intimidating, autocratic bully of a boss. Bill lies right at one end of a continuum, which I believe, represents the traditional view of leadership, characterised by what was seen as 'strong' leadership at one end and weak leadership at the other.

Bill is the extreme example of this perceived 'strong' leadership end of the continuum. There are many less

severe examples further down the continuum, but let's stick with Bill at the moment, because I think we probably all know a Bill.

Bills exist everywhere in organisations - not always right at the top, but wherever they are, they have got themselves into a job where they wield power through the position they hold. Bill has a simple philosophy that underpins his leadership beliefs. It goes something like this, 'the louder I shout at someone the more likely they are to do what I want them to do.'

At worst, Bill is a bully. When necessary he will intimidate people, humiliate them and put them down in order to get his own way. He is deeply rooted in 'win-lose' thinking - he believes that in order for him to win, someone else must always lose.

He is self-serving - it is all about him. He takes the credit when things go right, and makes sure he has someone else to blame when they go wrong. He constantly criticises others, never offers praise or recognition.

All in all, a very unpleasant person to work for. His team lives in constant fear, and feels unsupported and exposed. But at least they know where they stand, and often get on with the job. Some will try and ingratiate themselves with Bill, but others just keep their heads down.

Typically Bill's bosses like Bill. They are often 'Bill' themselves (maybe to a lesser degree, for this is the very end of the continuum), and Bill gets the job done for them. Bill does deliver results - but in the wrong way, and they are never sustainable.

Have you ever come across Bill? Most people I work with have at some time. Many are still bruised from the experience.

I completely accept that many people see Bill and his like as a strong leader, because he seems to get things done, to deliver results, and surely that is what leadership is all about? Well, I agree that leaders are there to deliver results, but they need to deliver them in the right way. With Bill, there is only one way - his way. Bill does have many followers, but all too often they are there because they feel they have no choice, not because they want to be. They rarely feel fulfilled, and he will never get the best out of them.

I don't agree that Bill is a 'strong' leader, certainly not my definition of strong. Bill is a bully and as we know, bullies are no more than cowards hiding behind the power they have taken from their position.

Not every boss with a predominantly autocratic leadership style lies as far to the extreme end of the continuum as Bill, but many still too often demonstrate his self-serving and autocratic traits. These are the people who always think their way is the right way, indeed the only way, and are not afraid to point it out to you!

There are leaders towards Bill's end of the continuum, who do seem to have many strengths, but they are mitigated by character weaknesses and behavioural traits. Many of them are famous. I think Steve Jobs, the late founder of Apple, was a great example. His genius, his innovative and creative ability, his achievements, are undeniable. If however, you read his excellent biography, you see the flawed genius emerging, the person who would treat his people with utter contempt and with the worst aspects of bullying behaviour.

I had the misfortune to work for a 'Bill' in the past. This guy was as autocratic as they come - and somewhat neurotic as well. At night, when everyone had gone home, he would tour our offices, reading the papers in our in trays.  In meetings he would target people - belittling them. He seemed to trust nobody. He got some results, his table thumping had people running this way and that, but everyone despised him. The working atmosphere was toxic. He sucked confidence and shattered self-esteem.

As Dwight Eisenhower said:

'you don't lead by hitting people over the head, that's assault, not leadership.'

At the other end of the continuum lies Sidney.

He is the absolute opposite of Bill. He is a really weak leader. He is completely incapable of taking a decision over anything. Never get behind Sidney in the canteen coffee queue. Your break will be over long before he has made his mind up between a latte or cappuccino.

Not only is Sidney completely indecisive, he cannot stand confrontation or controversy. When the going gets tough, you will find Sidney cowering behind the filing cabinet in his office.

Working for Sidney is as difficult as working for Bill. His team feels equally unsupported, lacking any clear direction, unable to get decisions made. It is also common that they will be tarred with the same brush as Sidney, their whole team being dismissed by others as being weak and ineffective.

At best, people who work for Sidney just decide to get on with it, to take decisions and to move things forward themselves. It is rarely a comfortable place to be. Freedom without a framework is not empowerment, but abandonment - as we shall explore in a later chapter.

Have you ever worked with a Sidney? Many people I know have. They still wince at the experience. 'Sidney' seems to pervade middle management roles, even senior roles in organisations - a real hindrance to progress.

I came across several Sidneys back in my corporate role. One had somehow been promoted to a senior role, responsible for new brand roll-outs. His decisions would determine the way the company moved forward and where investment would be placed. Unfortunately, he was incapable of making any! He dithered, he prevaricated and he resembled a rabbit in headlights in meetings. The roll-out stalled.

Amazingly, I came across this same Sidney again some years later, when I had a sales role. He was now in the senior operations role in a major UK theme park. Nothing had changed. I only wanted to sell him some beer but once more he was incapable of taking a decision. To this day, I have no idea how he managed to gain these big roles.

I do believe this continuum is how we have traditionally looked at leadership, with 'strong' leaders towards one end, weak leaders at the other end - all sorts of variations in between.

But there is a very different way to lead - an authentic leader, who gains their authority not from the position they hold, but because of who they are. One who demonstrates strong leadership in a very different way. These leaders are at the heart of an amazing leadership evolution.

It is time to meet Mary.

# Notes

# Chapter THREE
## Meet Mary

'Become the kind of leader that people
would follow voluntarily, even if you
had no title or position'

Brian Tracy

If Bill and Sidney lie at the extremes of what we have traditionally regarded as 'strong' and weak leadership, then Mary is a very different kind of leader indeed.

Mary is absolutely as committed to delivering results as Bill. The difference is, she wants to deliver the right results and she wants to deliver them in what she believes is the right way. She is a very genuine person, who strives all the time to do the right thing. She derives her authority, her legitimacy to lead, not from the position she holds, but from whom she is. She is an authentic leader and that authenticity comes from deep within her character.

I'm sorry if that term 'authentic leader' sounds like management speak.

Authenticity has been explored throughout history, from Greek philosophers to the work of Shakespeare. Bill George, in his 2003 book 'Authentic Leadership', identified four traits:

Authentic leaders are self-aware and genuine

Authentic leaders are mission driven
and focussed on results

Authentic leaders lead with their heart, not just their mind

Authentic leaders focus on the long-term

Mary may be at the head of an organisation, but she could equally be anywhere. She could be heading a team, in a front-line role, or in a voluntary position inside or outside work. Highly self-aware, she knows, whatever role she has, she is far from perfect as a leader. Mary knows that there is so much she could improve on and is often riddled with self-doubt. She has a constant yearning to improve, to become a more effective leader - every single day. Never tiring of learning, Mary is fascinated by the challenge of becoming a more effective leader.

Mary cares deeply about her people, and others she comes into contact with, whether they be her team, colleagues, people from other organisations, customers - whoever.

She also strives to lead effectively in her life outside work. She wants to make a positive impact, to do the right thing in supporting her family and friends and making a community contribution via her voluntary activities.

Mary is low in ego and high in humility. When things are going well, she wants those around her to take the credit. When things are going badly, she takes responsibility herself and strives to improve.

Deeply ingrained within her, is a belief that her first role is to serve those around her - it's what defines her as a leader. She seeks to give her team absolute clarity on what is expected of them - to give them the tools and resources to do their jobs, but also the right level of freedom to allow them to perform.

There is nothing soft about Mary. She is absolutely determined to succeed, but always through her people. She has enormous capacity to overcome set-backs, to pick herself up, dust herself off and find new ways of addressing challenges. Mary never shies away from taking hard decisions, but focuses on doing the right things to deliver the right results, in the right way.

If Mary sounds too good to be true, let me emphasise again, she is far from perfect. The Mary I have created here is a fictional character, but I work with and meet 'Mary' and those who aspire to be Mary, all the time - in many different roles throughout many different types of organisations. Mary has always existed- her characteristics and qualities are timeless.

I believe an evolution to a new kind of leadership is underway in many organisations and that authentic leaders, who strive to lead like Mary, are emerging.

Over the past few years, as I have worked with and observed countless leaders - some great, some good, some poor, some frankly disastrous, I have tried to assimilate what I believe are the common traits of the great leaders.

Those who are authentic leaders, determined to do the right things and to deliver the right results - those who lead like Mary. From these studies, discussions and analysis, common themes began to emerge which, over time, I have refined and tested.

I now feel at a point where I am confident to share this with you. I stress this is only my own thinking – for who am I to claim this is right? Indeed I do not believe there is one right answer to define great leadership. But I would love to share Mary's traits with you, to challenge you to consider your effectiveness as a leader, through self-analysis and reflection, against these traits.

Here are the ten traits I believe define Mary as a leader:

1.  She genuinely believes that her first role as a leader is to serve others

2.  She is personally highly effective

3.  She is 'values-led' and courageous

4.  She is both trusting and trustworthy.
    Through this she builds highly effective relationships

5.  She gets the right people on the bus,
    and the wrong people off.

6.  She is a visionary who executes

7.  She gives her people absolute clarity

8.  She gives her people freedom within a framework.
    She practices creative discipline

9.  She believes in and practices joint accountability

10. She is relentless

# Lead Like Mary Model:

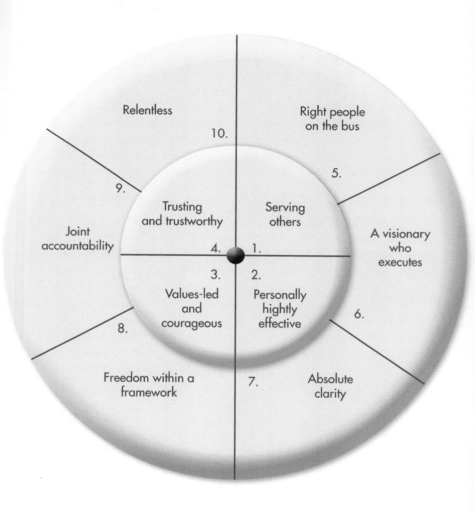

Illustrated in the 'Lead Like Mary' model, the first four of the traits lie deep within Mary's character.

They are within the inner circle of the Inside-Out Leadership model we explored in chapter 1.

These character traits define who Mary is as a leader.

They are where the leadership journey begins. As Norman Schwarzkopf remarked:

> 'Leadership is a potent combination of strategy
> and character. But if you must be without
> one be without the strategy'

If the first four traits are all about whom Mary is, the remaining six traits are about what she does - how she leads others around her. They are within the middle circle of the Inside-Out Leadership model. Mary's ability to effectively apply traits 5 – 10, come from the inner strength of the first four traits - deep within her.

In the rest of this book, we will examine each of these ten traits in turn. I will try to explain what I mean by each trait and give you practical examples and tools to demonstrate each one in action. In addition to referencing additional reading material, I end each chapter with self-reflective questions, all of which may assist you in considering your own effectiveness in relation to each of the traits. At the end of the book, I will point you in the direction of further support materials and tools.

I have included notes pages - I actively encourage you to write in this book - on those pages, or anywhere else! I hope this book remains a point of reference for you, throughout your leadership journey.

All I ask from you is an open mind, as together we explore the first trait.

So, let's consider Mary's deeply held belief that her first role as a leader is to serve others.

# Notes

# Chapter FOUR
## Serving Others

'If your actions inspire others to dream more, learn more, do more and become more then you are leader'

John Quincy Adams

'Leadership is a privilege to better the lives of others, It is not an opportunity to satisfy personal greed'

Mwai Kibaki

Let's begin the journey by exploring Mary's first trait. She deeply believes that her first role as a leader, is to serve others. She is low in ego and high in humility.

I thought very hard before including this as a trait. Do you really need to believe in serving others in order to be a highly effective leader? I know many good leaders who certainly do not have this belief, even some good leaders who I would describe as having a large ego. The more I study this and the more I work with truly great leaders, I find this trait emerging, time and time again. For me, it's the starting point of the whole leadership journey.

But what does serving others actually mean? First and foremost, it is not about being subservient. It's not about being at the beck and call of others, pandering to their every whim. Mary does not spend her days making countless cups of tea for her grateful team. She deeply believes that her role as a leader is to serve others, which she does by supporting them, giving clarity, listening and empowering them. She genuinely wants them to succeed, so ensures they have the necessary support, tools and freedom, to allow them to do so.

Mary is high in humility and low in ego. These were the traits of 'Level 5 Leaders' described by Jim Collins and his team in 'Good to Great.' They studied organisations that had enjoyed success over a sustained period of time, comparing them to other organisations in the same market sectors, which had failed to break through. They then identified common themes in the successful organisations not present in the comparison cases. One theme was around the leadership style of the person at the top - consistently found to combine personal humility with an absolute will to succeed, whatever the odds. This relentless element we return to later in this book - it is the final of Mary's traits.

I want to stress that these leaders can exist anywhere in organisations, not just the top. A leader can believe it is right to serve others and demonstrate this every day, in any role, from the boardroom to the front line. I work with 'Marys' and those who strive to lead like Mary, at every level, from junior roles to Chief Executives.

This commitment to serving others is the common thread

that binds these leaders together, whatever their role, at every level.

A friend of mine has a senior leadership role in the Scouts Association. Recently I visited him at the beautiful Gilwell Park, home of the world wide scouting movement. We wandered through the stunning grounds, where the spirit of Baden Powell is everywhere, chatting about leadership. My friend demonstrates his commitment to serving those around him on a daily basis, through his actions and behaviours. He also spoke with much pride about the one hundred thousand volunteers running the movement at the grass roots. One hundred thousand volunteer leaders, doing amazing things, at a local level!

Jakkie, my wife, is a leader who serves. She wouldn't recognise the term 'leader' as a description of what she does, but believe me, she is one. Every week she runs a community shop in our village, providing local food, a meeting place for people and small enterprise opportunities. Her contribution to addressing issues like rural isolation is a wonderful example of a leader serving others.

We often think of leaders as being 'those up there on the soapbox', always in the limelight, rallying people to the cause with powerful speeches. Collins found a very different story when he looked at 'Level 5 Leaders'. Many of them were high in humility, self-effacing people, who shirked the limelight. They had very low egos. They were quietly spoken, caring deeply that their teams were recognised for their successes rather than personally seeking the credit. Do not confuse ego with charisma – they are very different things.

Mary demonstrates this perfectly. People want to follow her, not because of what she is, but who she is. She is highly charismatic and engaging. She is authentic. She cares deeply about people and genuinely wants to serve them.

Bill has the ego, Mary the charisma.

I once had the privilege of meeting Terry Leahy when he was Chief Executive of Tesco. This was a man at the absolute top of his profession, leading the third biggest retailer in the world, the UK's largest private sector employer. He had led his company through a decade of unparalleled growth.

I only spoke with him for five minutes or so, but in those five minutes I felt like I was the most important person in his world. He came across as incredibly charismatic but self-effacing. Cynics might claim this was no more than an act. I disagree, as do many others who have met him and worked with him. As a leader, Leahy always seemed to keep a low profile. On leadership programmes, I would often ask if participants knew who he was. They rarely did. Compare this to some of the egotistical, attention seeking heads of other large companies. Leahy brings 'Level 5 Leadership' to life for me.

His recent book, 'Management in 10 Words', makes excellent reading, exploring what he believes delivered the success Tesco enjoyed. Many of his observations closely mirror Mary's traits. We will return to some of them later.

Many of Mary's other traits are grounded in her commitment to serving others. It is this belief that ensures she trusts her people, provides them with absolute clarity, gives them freedom within a framework and practices joint accountability. Of course, you cannot fake this belief. You either have it - or you don't. It comes from deep inside Mary's character.

The concept of servant leadership has been around for a long while. Robert Greenleaf first coined it in 1970. He believed that great leaders are motivated by the desire to serve others - a refreshing break away from leaders motivated by self-interest and the pursuit of power.

Greenleaf goes on to say that the best test of a 'servant-leader' is whether those who are served, grow as people. Now, there will be a view that in these difficult times, this is just too wishy-washy... that what we need is strong, decisive, even autocratic leaders, taking the hard decisions. There is nothing weak or indecisive about being a 'servant-leader.' Servant-leaders still make the tough decisions but ensure they are made for the right reasons and implemented in the right way.

This is an absolutely crucial point, and lies at the heart of Mary's character. There is nothing remotely weak about Mary, or any other leader who believes their first role is to serve others. Mary is strong and determined. She is no push over. She is absolutely committed to doing things in the right way.

In a 2005 essay, Larry Spears, who worked closely with Greenleaf, outlined the ten characteristics of a 'servant-leader' as follows:

1. The ability and willingness to listen to people

2. The determination to strive to understand and to empathise with others

3. The potential to heal (in organisational terms, the ability to resolve issues)

4. Being aware and understanding issues involving ethics and values - knowing right from wrong.

5. Able to persuade, seeking to convince others, rather than to coerce compliance

6. Able to think beyond today's realities and to conceptualise solutions to problems

7. Displaying foresight, the ability to predict the likely outcome of a situation

8. Stewardship, playing their role in holding their organisation in trust for the greater good of society

9. Commitment to the growth of each individual in the organisation

10. Seeking to find some means of building a community among those who work within an organisation

As we explore Mary's other traits in future chapters, we will see how closely they interweave with Spears work.

Mary's belief that her first role as a leader is to serve others translates into her feeling that she is doing truly important and worthwhile work. She does all she can to ensure that her team also feel their work is meaningful. Through this, she creates a sense of purpose for people. She also understands the crucial importance of delivering great customer service, whether to external or internal customers.

Some leaders, who genuinely believe they are there to serve others, have gone as far as to invert the classic hierarchical pyramid. No longer do they place themselves at the top, with successive layers of managers below them - right down to the bottom rung of front line people. Instead, they place themselves at the bottom, with front line staff right at the top. Now, a whole new culture of leadership can develop - one where each layer of management is focussed on serving those above them, by enabling them to perform effectively.

This does have to be genuine - the leader at the bottom of the hierarchy really does have to mean it. I've seen this done in organisations because it was the latest management fad. It looked great on a PowerPoint slide and on the annual report. Like so much else however, you can't fake it. Only authentic leaders, leaders like Mary, who deeply believe that their first role is to serve others, can make this really happen.

Perhaps more than anything, Mary understands that through serving others, she can make a difference - at every level. Making a difference does not need to mean achieving transformational organisational change everyday. Whatever Mary's role, whether she is at the head of an organisation, running a department, leading a small team, doing a front line job with no line management responsibilities, or helping within her community, she can make a difference to someone every day.

This is beautifully demonstrated in one of my favourite stories. It's about starfish.

*'The old man awoke just before sunrise, as he often did, to walk by the ocean's edge and greet the new day. As he moved through the morning dawn, he focused on a faint, far away motion.*

*He saw a youth, bending, reaching, flailing arms, dancing*

*on the beach, no doubt in celebration of the perfect day soon to begin. As he approached, he realized that the youth was not dancing on the bay, but rather bending to sift through the debris left by the night's tide, stopping now and then to pick up starfish, then standing, to throw it back into the sea.*

*He asked the youth the purpose of the effort. "The tide has washed the starfish onto the beach and they cannot return to the sea by themselves," the youth replied. "When the sun rises, they will die, unless I throw them back into the sea."*

*As the youth explained, the old man surveyed the vast expanse of beach, stretching in both directions beyond eyesight. Starfish littered the shore in numbers beyond calculation.*

*The hopelessness of the youth's plan became clear and the old man countered, "But there are more starfish on this beach than you can ever save before the sun is up. Surely you cannot expect to make a difference?"*

*The youth paused briefly to consider the old mans words, bent to pick up a starfish and threw it as far as possible. Turning to the man, he said,*

*"I made a difference to that one." '*

To me, the starfish story epitomises Mary.

Don't underestimate how genuine Mary is in her belief that her first role as a leader, is to serve others. It defines her, frames her purpose every single day, both inside and outside work. Her other traits flow from this belief and commitment.

A commitment to serving others on its own however, cannot be enough. To be an effective leader Mary must strive to be personally effective herself.

# Case Study

I coach and support someone who really does deeply believe that his first role as a leader is to serve others. He heads up operations on a very traditional production plant. He leads teams of shift workers, who work round the clock in an environment where stable, efficient production and an absolute adherence to safety, is of paramount importance.

Typically, people in his role come from a long line of 'Bills'. This certainly characterised many of his predecessors. This person however, is striving to lead in a different way. He believes that if he treats his people with respect, listens to them, supports them, gives them clarity, encourages them to come up with improved ways of working and recognises their achievements, he will get far more out of them.

He inherited a team a few years ago - low in morale, where negative attitudes prevailed, on a site which was under-invested in, run down, and threatened with closure. The journey has not been easy - old attitudes, deeply ingrained, die a slow death. Through his consistent actions, his resilience, and above all, his belief that he is leading in the right way, tangible change has occurred, both in attitude and behaviour. Slowly the culture has changed.

With this culture change, has come improved performance - one really has led to the other. This step change in performance has been recognised by the owners, monies have been made available for investment and the whole appearance of the site has improved, leading to greater pride. It is a virtuous circle.

This does not mean, of course, that it is all plain sailing. Every day brings new challenges, sometimes progress seems painfully slow, often it slips back, but the overall direction of travel is right. Leaders committed to serving others can deliver extraordinary changes.

## Self reflection

Think of leaders who you really admire. They might be famous, or just someone who has been a role model for you. Take a few minutes to write down what you regard as their qualities, their leadership traits.

What three words would people currently use to describe you as a leader? What three words would you **like** them to use? Is there a difference between the words? What could you do, to begin to narrow the gap?

How do you feel, deep inside you, about the concept of a leader who believes their first role is to serve others? How does it resonate with you? Is this a principle that makes sense for you, as you consider your own leadership journey?

## Further reading

'The Power of Servant Leadership' by Robert Greenleaf

'The Secret' by Ken Blanchard

The Level 5 Leadership chapter from 'Good to Great' by Jim Collins

# Notes

# Chapter FIVE
## Personally Effective

'We must be the
change we wish
to see in the
world'

Mahatma
Ghandi

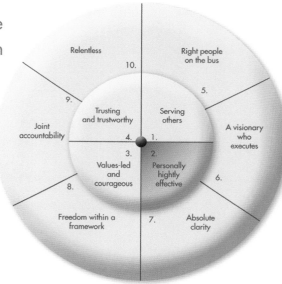

When I introduce Mary and describe her characteristics, some people get quite angry and frustrated. 'How', they ask, 'can one person ever be such a perfect leader? It's just not realistic'. I stress the point that I agree with them. In no way is Mary a perfect leader, she is far short of the finished article, even if that person could ever exist.

The point is, Mary knows that. She understands she is far from being the perfect leader. Her high level of self awareness allows her to recognise her flaws and to strive every day to improve.

Her low ego and high humility also means she is willing to ask those around her how she is doing and genuinely listen to, and act on the feedback. How can we strive to continually improve, if we never ask how we are doing?

Mary thinks deeply about her role as a leader. She knows if she leads in the right way, she will inspire her people and those around her. She recognises that unlocking their potential is the secret to them delivering amazing results.

She also understands, as we explored in the first chapter, that leadership is an inside-out activity. It starts in the inner circle - with how effective she is at leading herself. She knows it's the only place a leadership journey can begin. Only when she is effective in the inner circle, does she gain the ability and legitimacy to lead those around her in the middle circle. Mary's first four traits are all about leading herself, about the inner circle. They are character-based traits.

Mary understands that in order to become an effective leader of others, she must first be an effective leader of herself. She must take control of herself, and grow her personal effectiveness.

There are many models of personal effectiveness around, and we only have the space here to examine one in detail. It's the one I was introduced to maybe fifteen years ago. Back then, as I mentioned earlier, I was working in the private sector. I had reached the point where I was increasingly disillusioned. I was trying to find my way as a leader, but saw all too many poor examples around me, too few role models who I would aspire to. I was also going through a difficult period in my private life, after a personal tragedy and before meeting Jakkie. In so many ways my life was lacking in direction.

Unexpectedly, I received an invitation from a leader I did

admire, to attend a training programme, 'The Seven Habits of Highly Effective People'. Sceptical at first, thinking I was too busy to spare three days on some mumbo jumbo management training, I first declined, but then thought better of it. I was aware this particular leader had been running the programme for many of his people and I knew how much more positive and engaging the culture he had created seemed to be. So, with fairly low expectations, I went along.

I balk a little at using the words 'life changing' - they are overused words suggesting some kind of mystical conversion! It wasn't like that, but the whole programme just made total sense. The excellent facilitator challenged my beliefs, persuaded me to look at things differently, the material gave me a framework - a route map to strive to become more effective in all aspects of my life.

I am not for one moment suggesting that the '7 Habits' will have the same effect on everyone. This was a very personal thing and as things have the habit (excuse the pun) of doing, came at just the right point in my life, but I think there is enough in the material for anyone to make small changes - changes that help to improve effectiveness.

When I started working for myself, I got to know Stephen Covey's organisation in the UK, and became an associate facilitator for them. Now, I learned far more about the material and was able, for five years or so, to deliver it as a training programme to many people in a variety of organisations. This was a very fulfilling experience, particularly as I watched the impact it had on the people I delivered to, which ranged from occasionally genuinely life changing, through to thought provoking, leading to small improvements, to sometimes just cynical!
Covey first published the '7 Habits' way back in 1989.

It could, therefore be a justified argument that this is old stuff, the world has moved on, more modern thinking must have developed. This is what I love about the material - it is based on timeless principles of effectiveness - natural laws that are as relevant today as they were in 1989, as they always have been and always will be.

I also stress, whenever I present a personal effectiveness programme, I am not suggesting the people I am working with are ineffective. Of course they are not. If they were, they wouldn't be doing the jobs they are doing, living the lives they are living. Personal effectiveness, like so many other things, can be expressed as a continuum, with high effectiveness at one end, low at the other. We can all use our own self awareness to place ourselves on that continuum. Of course, we are never still - we move along in both directions, based on how much pressure we are under at certain times - how good the balance in our lives. When I present this material, I simply challenge people to think what they need to do to move a short way along the continuum, to become even more effective.

I'm not going to attempt to reproduce the '7 Habits' here. I hope you may be interested enough to get hold of the book for yourself, or to search on-line for the many excellent summaries of the material. The work is based around a series of principles, which are no more than common sense.

Some of Covey's '7 Habits' are concerned with the inner circle of 'inside-out leadership' - they are about how effective we are within ourselves. Covey calls it our 'private victory'. Other 'habits' are about building long-term, productive relationships with others - his 'public victory'. We shall return to the latter in a couple of chapters, when we consider Mary's trait of being trusting and trustworthy, through which she builds highly effective relationships.

I said that Covey's work is based on enduring principles of effectiveness, which are no more than common sense. All too often, common sense is not common practice. Mary recognises this and strives every day to become a little more effective. She has developed a framework to follow, based on Covey's work and what she's learned are the broad principles of effectiveness.

## Mary models the behaviours she wants to see in others

Mary is determined to behave in the right way. She also recognises a simple truth - why should she expect anyone else around her to behave in a certain way, unless they see her behaving that way herself?

She therefore constantly tries to model the behaviours she wants to see in others. She knows, for example, if her team see her working excessive hours, they will be far more likely to copy that behaviour. If she is not loyal to others, or talks negatively about them behind their backs, why would those around her be expected to behave any differently? She knows that as a leader, people are constantly watching how she acts and behaves.

Her behavioural framework is derived from her values, which we will examine in the next chapter. Modelling the behaviours she wants to see in others is captured wonderfully in the famous quote from Gandhi at the beginning of this chapter. We really must be the change we wish to see.

## Mary tries to keep an open mind and challenge beliefs

Every single one of us holds firmly embedded beliefs. They will be about how we feel about ourselves, our confidence, what we can achieve, our limitations. They will be about other people; our partner, family, friends, boss, work colleagues. They will be about aspects of our work and our organisation, about the world. These beliefs govern time and time again, how we act and behave. In turn our actions and behaviours govern the results we get, which in turn, re-enforces how we saw the situation to start with. If, for example, we feel there is no point in making suggestions on how to improve things at work, because no-one will listen to us and nothing ever changes, what are we going to do?

My guess is, we keep our heads down, because what's the point of suggesting improvements?

What happens? Nothing changes - which re-enforces our view that there was no point in making suggestions! It's a wicked circle of 'see-do-get' that goes round and round.

Obviously, not all the beliefs we have are wrong. Many are entirely correct, driving the right behaviours. We all also have limiting beliefs - they are preventing us from making progress in our lives.

Mary recognises that beliefs can be limiting, so tries to challenge herself and others to look at a situation differently and to encourage others to do so. She is self-aware, an endowment we all possess but many of us don't make use of anywhere near enough.

She also understands that if we want to really make changes, to deliver much improved results, to achieve a breakthrough, we can only do so when our beliefs change. Getting someone to act or behave differently, without changing their beliefs, will only ever bring small improvements.

Challenging your own beliefs and those of others, takes courage - a trait we shall return to later.

## Mary understands she can always make choices and strives to make the right choices

Mary deeply understands a basic principle of effectiveness - we always have a choice. So often, we come across people who simply react to situations, fly off the handle when something happens to them. They receive an e-mail that angers them and fire off a reply, without a second thought. They are criticised in a meeting, so react negatively. They are carved up by the driver in front, so react with clenched fist and at worst, a carve-up manoeuvre of their own. All of us know where that can lead - we read about the consequences every day - but many of us still find ourselves reacting.

Mary is not perfect. There are still certain circumstances where she knows she reacts, but she also understands we can always exercise choice, whatever the stimulus. We can leave a gap between that stimulus and our response. We can press a 'pause' button. We can exercise our 'freedom to choose.'

It's not easy to do this consistently - we all slip back - but really, understanding that choice always exists, can be a breakthrough moment for us as we strive to grow our effectiveness.

## Mary sets clear goals, at every level

Mary understands a simple principle of effectiveness around goal setting. It is no more complex than realising if we can envisage the outcome of something before we begin it, the chances of successful delivery will greatly increase.

It sounds so obvious. Surely everyone understands and applies this principle? I come across countless examples where people have failed to envisage outcomes before commencing a project, a new initiative, often resulting in unsuccessful outcomes.

The joy of this principle is that it can apply at every level, from the next meeting we are attending, to a forthcoming weekend or holiday with the family, a project we are about to commence, our next year at work or indeed, to crafting a broad plan for our lives.

Mary tries to envisage outcomes at every level and whenever appropriate, to involve those around her in creating the outcomes together.

*The principle of setting goals can apply at all levels, not just the next meeting you are attending or project you are leading. It can equally apply to setting life goals, creating a life plan. Whenever I mention those words to people, I get a variety of reactions. Some people recoil - setting life goals is a scary thought - it's far more pleasant to drift through life, accepting what comes along. Some are concerned that if they have a plan, it could result in them missing opportunities, whilst for others, it just makes sense.*

*I always stress that a life plan should not be too rigid. If it is, prepare to be disappointed and to miss opportunities. Just like the next meeting, if we have a broad plan of what we want to achieve over a much longer period of time, perhaps the chances of living a purposeful life and achieving our dreams, goals and ambitions, may greatly increase.*

*Take a few moments to consider the following questions:*

*How much of your potential (scored 0-10) do you believe you have realised in your life to date?*

*Which one great achievement is still inside you?*

*They may be deep and difficult questions, but they might also get you thinking about your future.*

*Now, let me take you forward to a future birthday of yours. One of those decade birthdays that ends in a zero. Not the next one - the one ten years after that. So, if you are in your thirties, it's your fiftieth birthday, and so on. What do you want your life to be like as you look around you on that birthday? It's still a vague question, so let's give it a bit of structure. Break it down into 'have, do and be.' When you reach that day what do you want to have in your life, to be doing and to have done, what kind of person do you want to be?*

**Have:** *at first this may seem a bit materialistic. It may well include tangible things you want to have in your life on that future day, such as property, possessions and wealth, but it may well also include thoughts on your health. Very few of us would choose to be in poor health on that birthday. There are no guarantees that we will reach that day in robust health, but I wonder, could we do a little more from today, to give us at least more of a chance of that? I also suspect that in thinking about what we want to have in our lives when we reach that future birthday, many of us will use words like 'happiness, fulfillment, contentment, love'. Very few of us would be likely to choose the contra words. What do we need to focus on doing from today, what decisions do we need to take, to make those hopes a reality?*

**Do:** *look around you at that future birthday. What are you doing in your life? In broad terms (remember, do not be too prescriptive) where are you in terms of job and career? Are you doing voluntary work, what hobbies and interests are you pursuing? What are you doing with family and* friends? Now, look back - what have you done over the past few years? What have been the highlights of your professional life - what difference have you made? Did you realise the 'great achievement' you considered above? Where have you travelled to, what special times have you enjoyed with family and friends? What memories do you cherish most? What new skills have you mastered?

**Be:** we finish by going deeper - what kind of person do you really want to be? Now for a bit of visualisation. Find somewhere quiet and imagine on this future birthday, a special party has been arranged to celebrate your landmark 'big zero' day. Look around you, see your family, friends, work colleagues, people important to you from all aspects of your life. The people you would want to spend that special day with. One after another, those people are going to stand up and talk about you. They want to tell others gathered there, why you are important to them - what difference you have made to their lives, why you are such a special person. Listen carefully, you can hear the words they say. When they finish speaking, you might even choose to write down some of the things they said. Now here's the challenge. Would they say those things about you today or do you need to focus even more on becoming the person you really want to be?

If you did all of the above and built up a picture of the future, would the journey from today to that future birthday be smooth? Of course not. Things will happen, happy and sad, which will knock you off course. New opportunities will present themselves, you will encounter new people on the journey. When we are knocked off course, having a plan will allow us to refocus and it will be broad enough to allow us to absorb changes.

Life planning is not for everyone but it just might be the secret to living an even more purposeful life.

Mary manages her time as effectively as she can, focussing on what is truly important

Whenever I run a personal effectiveness programme, I ask those present what is the one thing they know they need to improve, to become even more personally effective. By far, the most popular answer is quite simple - better time management.

People complain that they do not have enough hours in a day, they face constant interruptions, other people are stealers of their time, they spend far too long in pointless meetings or dealing with hundreds of irrelevant e-mails. Sound familiar?

I often ask people if they would benefit from having a couple more hours every day. They readily agree, but after reflection, accept they would probably only fill it with another couple of pointless meetings! It's not about the time you have, it's about what you do with that time. It's about discipline, prioritisation and personal organisation.

Mary works hard to manage her time effectively. She understands the importance of maintaining a broad work-life balance. She knows if she chooses to spend a maximum number of hours a week working, she must make those hours as effective as possible.

She does so by striving to adhere to just four principles for the effective management of our time.

Firstly, she tries to stay in control of herself - to maintain some kind of overall balance - to make choices over the hours she works.

Of course, there are times when she puts in excessive hours, where she is rushing here and there, keeping multiple plates spinning, she understands in the real world it is sometimes inevitable, but also, it is not sustainable and she needs to keep a broad level of control.

Secondly, she does all she can to focus on what is truly important. She understands we can all too often be sidetracked by things that are important to others, but not to us. These are merely urgent things - our greatest time stealers. She has taken the time to ensure she and her team know what their most important things are. We will see this process in action in a later chapter.

To help her she uses Covey's simple four-quadrant time management matrix, categorising activities based on their relative importance and urgency.

She then adopts a principle of weekly planning. She understands that no matter how valuable daily 'to do' lists are, they too often result in us focussing on doing the quick things, the urgent tasks, the easy activities, rather than those hard things, which take time.

Those things, usually important but not urgent - writing that strategy paper, carrying out a review with one of our team, kick starting a new project - are all too often the things that take us forward. So, every week she carefully plans the week ahead, allocating sufficient time in her schedule for those really important things.

Finally, she tries every day to work in a disciplined way, to do what she committed to doing, to deliver her plan for the week. She then reviews her effectiveness at the end of each week.

Some weeks are far from perfect. Mary understands that is inevitable, she just tries to make small improvements, week after week.

**She constantly acts to re-energise herself.**

Mary recognises that to remain effective she must constantly seek to re-energise herself. Only if she does so, can she remain in the best possible position to deliver, every day. We can re-energise in four ways, by focusing on our physical, mental, social and spiritual needs.

We can do so in a variety of ways. We can physically renew through exercise, yoga, meditation, care over what we eat and drink and getting enough sleep. Mental renewal could involve taking up a new hobby, learning a new language, reading, study, stimulating conversation. Social (and emotional) renewal might mean taking special time out with your partner and family, catching up with those friends you have lost contact with, getting out more, taking time to say 'thank you' to people.

Spiritual renewal is what it means to you - we are all unique individuals - it could be found by a walk in the countryside, some beautiful music, through religion or by spending time reflecting on our values and what is really important to us in our lives.

These principles give Mary a framework for personal effectiveness. It takes hard work every single day to apply them, to reflect and to improve.

Building and maintaining our personal effectiveness lies deep within us. So do our values and our inner courage, which we shall turn to next.

# Case Study

I first met a senior manager in a charity on a leadership programme I was running a few years ago. It soon became apparent in conversations both in and between sessions, she was facing many challenges and frustrations at work. She did not feel her boss was as effective as he could be, her senior manager colleagues were not working as an effective team and there were issues around trust, focus and team working throughout the organisation. In summary, this was a good organisation, doing important work, which had lost its way, where leadership was far from effective.

It soon became apparent this manager wanted to make changes, had a desire to improve things, but just didn't believe that she could make a difference. She felt helpless, wanting to change things but with no confidence that she could do so.

I saw real leadership potential in this person, even though she could not, at that point see it in herself. This lack of self-belief, lack of confidence, was driving how she was acting and behaving, determining the results she was getting, which simply re-enforced her beliefs. I saw a natural leader, who could make a real contribution, who could be at the forefront of organisational transformation. She had to see that for herself. She had to undergo a belief change.

At subsequent workshops, I therefore focussed on helping this manager to look at the situation differently. To examine her own beliefs. I did so through elements of the formal material we covered, but also through informal mentoring between sessions. Colleagues from other organisations on the programme also played their full part.

Gradually, over time, I saw her beliefs change. There was no one dramatic moment, no revelation, but she began to realise that maybe she could be the catalyst for change in her organisation through her leadership. She strived to do the right things with her team, to lead across the organisation with her colleagues and crucially, to try to lead upwards, to support her boss, but also to challenge him to change and to lead more effectively.

This is not a story with a perfect ending. Real life and real organisations are rarely like that, but I have watched this manager blossom as a leader - she is making a genuine difference. There are small steps forward everyday and of course, many steps back, with occasional crises of confidence, but the overall direction of travel is undeniable.

## Self reflection

Consider the beliefs you have about yourself, whether it's to do with your confidence, your abilities, your potential. Could any of them be limiting beliefs, holding you back from making progress?

Could you challenge those beliefs, look at things in a different way - could that help you realise your potential?

How good is your work-life balance? What could you do to restore that balance?

Where are you spending your time during a typical working week? Are you focussed enough on important things, or are you distracted by things that are merely urgent to you, even though they may be important to others? What can you do, to focus more time on those truly important things?

**Further reading:**

'The Seven Habits of Highly Effective People' by Stephen R Covey

# Notes

# Chapter SIX
## Values-Led and Courageous

'It's not hard to make decisions when you know what your values are'

Roy Disney

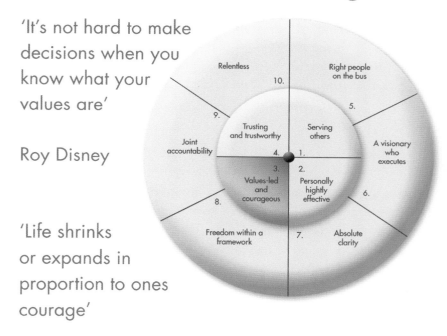

'Life shrinks or expands in proportion to ones courage'

Anais Nin

At first it might seem that we are trying to squeeze two separate things into Mary's third trait, but I really do believe that they are completely interdependent. It is being values-led that gives Mary the courage and moral framework to try always do the right thing. Mary is both values-led and courageous.

**What do I mean by values-led?**

1. Mary has a set of deeply rooted beliefs - her most

important principles. She strives, in her whole life, both inside and outside work, to act and behave in line with these principles, constantly and consistently. They form her bedrock whenever a difficult situation arises, or she needs to make a tough decision. She also understands that she must constantly role model those behaviours and values, if she is to expect anyone else to behave in the same way.

2. She is committed to ensuring that teams she leads and if appropriate, her whole organisation, has in place a values framework, which guides both decision making and individual behaviours.

We shall return to both of these points later.

Mary's beliefs lie deep inside her character, as do each of her first four traits. These aren't techniques, tricks that can be quickly learned, she can't fake them. They are fundamental to what makes Mary an authentic leader.

I am frequently asked the question 'are great leaders born or made?' I honestly don't know, but my instinct tells me that over our lives, things happen to us that can fundamentally change our views and beliefs - enabling us to achieve transformational change in the way we act and behave.

To illustrate this, I would like to share with you my experiences and how I think I changed my beliefs about leadership. Let me build on the brief introduction to my background I gave you, back in Chapter 1.

In my early twenties I somehow got the job as the senior staff member of a small charity. It was my first job after leaving University. There were only about ten or fifteen staff, but I was the boss, and therefore I really was thrown in at the deep end. I had no past experience on which to base my approach to leadership and management.

I basically bluffed my way through, learning each day by making many mistakes. Somewhere deep inside me, I knew I loved working with and leading people and teams, wanting to give them the freedom to develop and unlock their potential, but back then, I couldn't have described that in any theoretical leadership way.

At 30, I took the decision to move into a large corporate organisation to broaden my experience and for the next fifteen years or so worked for that company in the leisure industry. I followed a classic upward career path in those years, spending a year or two in a role before being promoted onwards. Now I began to learn about leadership and how to manage people, not, on the whole, from training courses, but from a succession of bosses. The problem was, looking back with that wonderful gift of hindsight, I was learning how not to lead and manage people.

The best way I can describe the culture pervading that large organisation - the leadership mantra - was 'the louder you shout at someone, the more likely they are to do things'. Sound familiar from earlier in the book? Of course it does, the place was full of 'Bills'!

I witnessed (again with hindsight) appalling examples of this management style in action, also experiencing behaviour that could, at worst, be described as bullying. Here's the problem - I began to believe this was the right way, indeed the only way, to lead. Surely it was right if my boss did it? Their boss did it too - it was all around me. I am sorry to admit that I started to behave in this way as well. Results followed, they always will, if you shout loud enough, things do get done. The challenges being, are they the right things, and are they sustainable?

Over time, I became aware of one or two people in senior

levels in the company who seemed to lead in a different way. When I spoke to people who worked for them, they seemed genuinely inspired by their bosses. I began to challenge whether this was the only way to lead, to realise that, if you treated people in the right way, if you tried to unlock their potential, they would do amazing things in return. It took time, but it slowly dawned on me that there was another way to lead. I began to try to do so, with my team. It wasn't easy, I was frequently criticised by my bosses for being a weak manager (a Sidney). Those people equated caring about people with weakness. I also knew that even if I couldn't make the changes I desired at an organisational level, I could protect and influence my own team, try to lead them in the right way.

If there was one moment that drove transformational change in me, it was an incident with tragic consequences, in which I am convinced bullying was a major factor. I'm not going to dwell on it here, but often it takes a dramatic event to change beliefs and drive transformational change.

That spurred me on to grab the chance to be part of a sell off business from this big corporate. Myself, along with some like-minded people, spent a roller coaster but immensely fulfilling two years leading a business of a thousand retail units - in what we believed was the right way. Just as in my twenties, we made a lot of it up as we went along, but our commitment to create the opposite culture to that we had just left, at least gave us a broad framework.

I didn't know it at the time, but I was basing my leadership on a set of values, along the lines of fairness, integrity, treating people correctly, communicating brilliantly and joint accountability. These are the beliefs, which over a decade later, lie at the heart of my teaching and my business.

So, all I am trying to demonstrate with my story, is that we can change and develop over time. We can change our views, challenge what we believe in, learn from others and from experiences both good and bad and become a much more effective leader as a result.

Over the past few years, I have had the privilege to work with more and more leaders who really are values-led. They base their decision making, particularly when times are tough, on their most important values, or guiding principles. This is exactly what Mary does. Her values include fairness, integrity, trust, the belief that everyone is an individual, that it is always possible to unlock potential, that people should be supported, but in turn should be held accountable for doing what they say they are going to do.

There's an important point here. Sometimes, when we think about values, we assume we are talking just about 'soft' things like trust, integrity, fairness and honesty. These are important, but it is equally the case that our values could and should include things like accountability, innovation and a focus on the customer. Many 'Marys' I know and work with, would count such beliefs amongst their values.

So, for example, if someone is underperforming, Mary will never ignore the issue. She will deal with it in a fair way. She will ensure the person has the support they need, but if they still fail to deliver, she will take decisive action, but always with openness and honesty.

When times are tough and costs need to be reduced, she will not duck the issue. She will take the tough actions necessary to reduce costs, but always by open communication, involving her people in what needs to happen, being transparent, but also being determined. This lies at the heart of the 'Level 5 Leadership', described as part of Mary's first trait - someone who combines personal humility with professional will - who is fair but relentless. Mary frequently challenges herself against her values. When she reviews how she has done over the previous week, she not only considers the results she has delivered, but also, has she achieved those results in the right way? Has she done the right thing? Has she been consistent? She deeply believes that it's not just about what you do, but how you do it.

Mary really tries to role model these values and behaviours with others; her team, her colleagues, her boss, her customers. She is not afraid to ask them how she is doing. She wants to know, it's the only way she can improve. She often makes mistakes, and slips back. Mary is not perfect, but she strives to improve all the time.

If you want to read more about values-based leadership, there is a great book by a guy called James Despain entitled 'And Dignity for All, Unlocking Greatness with Values-Based Leadership'. His story resonates with my own experiences. He worked for Caterpillar in the United States and was brought up in a culture of rough, tough, no nonsense management. Knowing no other way, this was how he led. He was put in charge of a failing plant, and found his approach would just not work. He dramatically changed his leadership style, transforming a struggling organisation into one based on values of respect, dignity, self-worth and innovation. It's a really powerful, true story.

At another level, Mary also understands that teams and even organisations can really prosper, if they develop their own set of organisational or team values, underpinned by a behavioural framework.

In his book 'Management in Ten Words', Terry Leahy summarises the importance of organisational values as follows;

'Strong values underpin successful businesses. They give managers a sheet anchor, something that holds their position and keeps them from being smashed against the rocks when caught in a storm. Values govern how a business behaves, what it sees as important, what it does when faced with a problem.'

Remember, 'Marys' can exist anywhere in organisations, from the front line to the board room. Many 'Marys' cannot change things at an organisational or even team level, it's outside their circles of control and influence. Nothing however, stops them acting in line with their own values.

Where they can make change at a team level, they have worked with their people to create the values and behavioural framework. It has become an integral and crucial part of the framework under which the team operates and thrives. It has even been embodied into a team charter.

These values must be developed by the team themselves - they can never be imposed. Some years ago, I was asked to work with teams on a manufacturing site. It was quickly clear that there were a myriad of issues, particularly around trust, respect and fairness. Frankly, some of the behaviours I witnessed, by managers, unions and front line staff, were appalling. I came across a set of values on a poster on the wall - all the predictable stuff around integrity, listening and accountability. No one even noticed they were there, let alone cared about them, or tried to behave in line with them. Where had they come from? Head office by e-mail, as a diktat. A disaster!

Equally, I have supported leaders and teams through a process of joint development of values and behaviours. Where it works, it delivers a transformational change in effectiveness. In those great teams and organisations, a major point of principle has been established. They regard how someone behaves, as being as important as what they do and deliver. They have incorporated this into systems and processes, such as recruitment and appraisals. There will be more on this in a later chapter, as we examine the trait of getting the right people 'on the bus'.

Values are subtly different at an organisational level. Here, I believe they are about the guiding principles that are most important for an organisation. The things it will never lose sight of, those things deeply rooted in their DNA. Many organisations I work with have incorporated these principals into their strategic plan and in the best examples, make those values live, whenever an important decision needs to be made. They seek to ensure that everything the organisation does, is in line with those values.

Again, at an organisational level, values must include 'hard' as well as 'soft' areas of focus. Of course organisations should demonstrate integrity, but they also need to be innovative to survive. Both are worthy values. So is an absolute focus on the customer.

Every organisation has customers - in whichever sector they operate. Sometimes, we give those customers different names, but they are still real people who use the goods or services. This applies equally to a charity, the NHS, a local authority, as it does to a private sector business. I truly believe that when great organisations put customers at the centre of everything they do, this becomes a fundamental value.

Remember that for many people in organisations, the

customer will be internal ones, people in other departments or functions. I would suggest that these customers are equally as important as external ones.

Putting the customer at the centre is a very easy thing to say. It is much more difficult to make it happen, every day, in every decision. There are organisations however, who really mean it - who live that value, who bring it to life, who base their decision-making around that simple concept. This really does transform how they behave and what they do - with amazing results.

In truly highly effective organisations, values at an organisational level flow down into both team, and individual behaviours. That's where it really joins up and if Mary is leading an organisation she will strive to achieve that.

It is being 'values-led', that gives Mary the bedrock on which to be courageous. Leadership is not easy - every day there are obstacles and barriers. There are constant challenges to overcome.

Great leadership requires great courage to rise to these challenges and meet them head on. Mary often has to make unpopular decisions, difficult ones, which affect people's lives. She constantly tests those decisions against her values. Is she doing the right thing, in the right way? What is the right thing to do? This gives her a point of reference and the courage and determination needed, to lead both fairly and effectively.

To quote Aristotle:

'Courage is the first of human qualities,
because it is the quality that guarantees all the others'

History is full of amazing stories of famous leaders who demonstrate great courage in adversity. Leadership isn't about being famous. Day in, day out 'Marys' everywhere take courageous decisions, decisions that affect lives, deal with issues, resolve differences, build effectiveness.

Organisations need to be courageous if they are to prosper. Terry Leahy summarises courage at this level as follows:

'Good strategies need to be bold and daring. People need to be stretched to do more than they think. Goals have to cause excitement and perhaps just a little fear. Above all, they need to inspire and present an organisation with a choice: have these great ambitions, or remain as you are.'

I cannot stress enough, that there is nothing weak about leading like Mary. She wants to be fair in all that she does. Being fair, being values-led, is an amazing strength, never a weakness. I think it's the strongest form of leadership there is.

Just a word on decision making. Compare Mary's approach to that of Bill and Sidney. Bill is quick to make a decision. He doesn't hang around. He tells people what to do. Some people really do admire that trait. He is decisive. The decision is always based on what he wants, however, not necessarily on what is right. He never listens to other people. Sidney on the other hand, seems incapable of making a decision. He seems to listen to people, but never really hears them. He sways this way and that, changing his mind based on whom he last spoke to and decisions never emerge. He is the king of prevarication.

Mary is always willing to listen to others before making

a decision. She respects their points of view, wants to understand them. They inform her decision making, but she is never dictated to, by their views. She makes up her own mind based on what she has heard, but also on her values. She knows the right thing to do. She does not prevaricate. When she has made the decision, she gets on with it, she does not waver - she sees things through. She is both courageous and determined. To me, that's what decision making is all about.

Mary does strive to be courageous but it's never easy. She could never be described as over-confident, indeed often suffers from a lack of confidence. 'Can I really do that? Is it the right thing to do? What if I mess up?'

Mary has learned to give it a go - to step out of her comfort zone. She has learned that she can always 'fake it 'til you make it'. She may be gripped with nerves, when making a presentation, addressing a large audience, or dealing with a particularly difficult people issue, but doesn't duck the responsibility or the challenge. She gets up there and gives it a go, even though her confidence may at first, be an act. The more she has a go, the more confident and competent she becomes.

'Fake it 'till you make it'. I love it! When I was eighteen our communist leaning Latin teacher (he drove a Lada which was all the proof I needed), Mr Ludlow, hired a coach and took forty of us on the 1970s equivalent of a grand tour of Europe.

He fulfilled his life's ambition to visit the (then) Soviet Union. It was a catalogue of disasters. We got hopelessly lost in a Finnish pine forest, spent eight hours at the Soviet border having our coach literally taken apart bolt by bolt, ran out of fuel somewhere north of (then) Leningrad, managed to insult our KGB minder with our drunken antics, then came within a hairs breadth of the whole coach being arrested for insulting the East German nation at Checkpoint Charlie!

Through it all however, Mr Ludlow maintained a calm demeanour, coping with every crisis as it occurred, (probably helped by copious amounts of vodka), getting us all home safe and sound, with enriched minds, if dodgy livers! Vic Ludlow, I salute you - you were one of my first role model leaders.

Mary's deep-rooted principles guide her decision-making and provide a moral framework from which she is courageous and relentless in her quest to do the right thing. Being trustworthy and trusting others are examples of those deeply rooted principles. Let's examine those next.

# Case Study

Over the past few years I have worked with two leaders, in very different sized organisations, both of whom are truly values-led. I choose to support both leaders on a voluntary basis, primarily because of my admiration for who they are and how they lead.

The first, heads up a very small organisation whose focus is finding employment opportunities for people with disabilities. She is a really extraordinary person, who puts her heart and soul into her work. From the first moment I met her, I was aware of the importance to her of having a strong values framework - both for herself and for her team. She has developed these values with her team, keeps them front of mind for everyone - her decision making is firmly and consistently rooted in these values.

The last few years have been very difficult for this leader, with the economic downturn leading to the loss of major contracts. The loss of income has resulted in the need to downsize and to re-examine not only strategy, but the very purpose and existence of her organisation. Through all of these difficult times, I have observed a constant referral to her values framework, which has acted as a bedrock and beacon for her decision making.

The other leader heads up a much larger organisation, doing important work in the voluntary sector. Values-led herself, this leader has deeply immersed a set of values throughout her organisation. They form a framework for how people are expected to behave. She has gone a stage further however, integrating these values into a whole series of systems and processes, including recruitment, performance management and reward structures. When recruiting new people, everything possible is done to ensure a 'values fit' between the candidates and the organisation. It's seen as being at least as important as that person's ability to do the job. It doesn't always guarantee successful recruitment, but at the very least it increases the chances of having the right people (in every way) stepping aboard the bus.

Strong adherence to values has enabled both of these leaders to make courageous decisions in difficult times and build strong organisations.

## Self reflection

Think deeply about your own values. What are the most important things to you? Can you articulate them? Can you draw up your own values framework?

Commit that you will constantly seek to live those values. To role model the behaviours which bring those values to life. To use those values as your moral framework, whenever a difficult decision needs to be made. Review as part of your weekly planning. How well did you live your values over the past week? What could you have done better?

Think through the big decisions you have made in your life in your recent past. Have you demonstrated courage in those decisions, always sought to do the right thing, based on your values? On reflection, what would you have done differently? What will you do differently in the future? What big decision have you been putting off, which needs to be acted on?

## Further reading

'And Dignity for All, Unlocking Greatness with Values-Based Leadership.' James Despain

'Management in Ten Words' Terry Leahy

# Notes

# Chapter SEVEN
## Trusting and Trustworthy

'Trust people and they will be true to you. Treat them greatly and they will show themselves great'

Ralph Waldo Emerson

'Long-term, highly effective relationships require mutual respect and mutual benefit'

Stephen R Covey

Mary's fourth trait - she is both trusting and trustworthy, through which she builds long-term, highly effective relationships.

This particular trait is the last of those that I believe are character based - coming from deep inside Mary. This trait, together with believing her first role as a leader is to serve others - being personally highly effective, values-led and courageous - is what defines Mary as a person and makes her an authentic leader. The remaining six traits, from the next chapter onwards, are about what Mary does as a leader.

Being trusting and trustworthy are, of course, values which Mary holds deeply. These values could therefore, have been incorporated into the values-led trait we have just explored. For me, however, these values are such significant leadership traits, that I believe it is appropriate they stand on their own.

Mary is highly trusting of others. This is an important trait, and one which, in my experience, is both rare and hard to practice consistently and effectively. I think so often we are suspicious of the motives of others and tend to be slow to trust. We are too often like a card player, keeping our cards very close to our chest, convinced that if we show even a little, we will quickly be taken advantage of and maybe even cheated.

There is of course, a fine line to tread here, which great leaders develop over time. Unless we are willing to trust others, we cannot make progress. Equally, we are going to ensure that we do not extend trust over a period of time, to those who do not deserve it. Being trusting is not a weak position to take. Mary will quickly take appropriate action if she senses her trust is being exploited.

Mary also understands deeply, trust lies at the heart of every effective relationship. Outside work this is obvious - the higher the trust between partners in a marriage or relationship, the more fulfilling that relationship. The same applies between parents and children and between friends. Think of your own relationships outside work, where trust is high or where trust is low and consider the differences between those relationships.

Mary also understands that the same principles apply at work. Here, she also has many relationships. She is a boss, a team member, a colleague, an internal customer, an external partner, maybe a supplier. She knows that where trust is high, things get done. She does not need to be continually checking back with people to see if they are doing what they said they would. She knows that where trust is high, people are honest, their intent is genuine and they will deliver the right results in the right way.

She is willing to give people the benefit of the doubt, to extend to them a first level of trust, even if she does not yet know if it is justified. She has found that if she is willing to show people a card or two, many times her trust will be rewarded. Although it is her first inclination, she does it with care and will never accept her trust being abused. She believes deeply in accountability (we explore this as a later trait) and will always deal firmly and effectively with a situation where her trust has been let down.

Mary is also trustworthy. This comes right back to her values-led trait. She is high in integrity, and goes out of her way to demonstrate through her behaviours and actions, that she can be trusted. She knows that trust lies at the heart of everything.

Trust is not just about integrity. In his excellent book 'The Speed of Trust' Stephen M R Covey (son of the '7 Habits' man) examines trust at four levels; two linked to character and two to competence. When we trust someone we can trust their integrity and intent (character based), and their capability and results (competence based). Mary works hard to prove her trustworthiness in each of those four areas.

In the book Covey demonstrates the absolute and undeniable link between the level of trust in a team or organisation and the ability of that team or organisation to execute - to get things done. When trust is high, speed goes up and costs go down and the opposite occurs when trust is low.

This is a convincing argument and although it may seem obvious, in my experience, it is not a link that is understood by many leaders. For too many people, trust is still seen as a soft concept, which does not sit easily with the daily grind for results. It might be there on the wall as a values statement, but it is seen as the domain of HR rather than being central to effectiveness and results.

Covey makes the link brilliantly. He talks about a 'trust tax' and a 'trust dividend'. When trust is low it is a tax on your effectiveness, it slows things down. When trust is high it becomes a dividend, speeding things up. He goes further, demonstrating the economic benefit of high trust, supported by compelling evidence.

To bring this to life, when I work with groups on these principles I ask them to think of a relationship they have at work (with any stakeholder such as a customer, a colleague, a team member, another department, even their boss) where trust is high, and one where trust is low. I ask them to consider how the relationship works in practice. Specifically, the effects that high or low trust have on the ability to get things done. The answers are obvious and come thick and fast. When trust is high, decision-making is easy - people are allowed to get on with things - we do not need to keep checking up on people. We can empower, confident that we will get results. When trust is low, the opposite occurs and things take so much more time to get done.

Covey describes in detail five levels of trust: self, relationship, organisational, market and societal.

He also, crucially, demonstrates that any leader can build trust. So, if you have taken over a team or organisation where trust is low, where there is a large trust tax, or if you simply recognise the need to build trust in your existing team or organisation, Covey expands on thirteen principles of behaviour for building trust. Once more they come across as little more than common sense, but I watch highly effective leaders I already work with, demonstrate these behaviours constantly. A good book - well worth a read if you want to explore trust further.

It is through being both trusting and trustworthy that Mary builds long-term, highly effective relationships. She recognises that all of us, at work and outside of work, are involved in a whole series of relationships. We are a boss, colleague, team member, business partner, coach, mentor, friend, husband, wife, son, daughter, parent. The more effective the relationships, the more likely we are to deliver great results. She understands that it takes time to build great relationships and is willing to invest that time. She also understands that long-term, highly effective relationships require mutual respect and mutual benefit. It is through these relationships that Mary gets things done.

Once more, Mary turns to the older Covey's '7 Habits', for a powerful framework for building and maintaining great relationships everywhere. Inspired by Covey's work, she has developed her own thinking based on these timeless principles of effectiveness.

**Great relationships do not just happen, they require constant attention and effort.**

They do indeed, but let's leave relationships for a moment. I'd like you to think about your bank account - your current account. There are two primary transactions in that account. Money goes in and it comes out. Not always in equal proportions! What happens if the withdrawals we make from our bank account significantly exceed the deposits? Well, for a start, we would go overdrawn, which could lead to letters from the bank, a withdrawal of further credit, it might affect our credit worthiness. It could also lead to stress, arguments, even depression. Ultimately, if it keeps happening, we could go bankrupt.

In exactly the same way as we have a bank account for our salary to be paid into, we also have one with every person with whom we have a relationship. Indeed, there are two bank accounts, they have one with you, you have one with them. In exactly the same way as you can make deposits in your real bank account, you can make them in these relationship bank accounts. What deposits can you make? Well, you can listen to people, support them, care for them, teach them, love them, do them favours, enable them… the list is endless. We can also make withdrawals from their bank accounts, many of which would be doing the opposite of the deposits above. If the withdrawals we make significantly exceed the deposits, relationships can go into overdraft, leading to stress and anxiety. This could also affect our credit worthiness elsewhere - just like in our real bank account.

So, relationships need working at. We can choose to place deposits into other people's bank accounts everywhere, every day. Think about your various relationships, both inside and outside work. Which have a high level of deposits, which are around nil balance, which have slipped into overdraft? Where do you need to focus on rebuilding deposits? Is it in your relationship with your partner, a friend you have lost contact with, a work colleague, your boss, a customer?

Mary understands this principle and tries every day to focus on making consistent deposits. It's not easy, especially if few deposits are flowing back in return, but it has to start somewhere.

## Relationships flourish where there is mutual benefit

Mary also understands the importance of mutual benefit in relationships. She knows that if both sides can win from an interaction, there is much more chance of building long-tem relationships.

To enable this to happen, Mary has a win-win mentality. She goes out of her way to seek a win for the other party, as well as one for herself. This is a very different mindset to one of 'win-lose' which unfortunately we come across all too often, inside and outside work. Think of Bill, determined to win at all costs, and destroy those around him, of the salesman determined to complete the deal even if it's not in the customer's interest, the relationship with a partner which has hit bad times and become vindictive and manipulative.

So, what does it take to think win-win and to deliver win-win outcomes? It takes courage, understanding, the willingness to listen, an open mind, creativity, exploration of options and time.

There is nothing weak about having a win-win mentality. It's in those words. Looking for win-win outcomes does not mean Mary will be willing to lose, to give too much away. She has the courage to strive to deliver mutual benefit. She knows that great relationships are dependent on it.

## We must be willing to listen, if we want to understand

I believe that listening is the least developed of our senses. If we really want to build great relationships, we must be able to understand another person's point of view. We can only build that understanding, if we are willing to properly listen.

So, what gets in the way of really effective listening? Lots of things, which is why it is so hard! Interruptions, distractions, cultural differences, time pressures, all of these are real obstacles to listening, but perhaps the biggest barrier of all, is ourselves. How many times do we fail to listen effectively, because we have already made up our mind about the other person? Our prejudices and our previous experiences, have already closed our minds. 'Here they come again, trotting out the same old stuff, they are so boring!'

Or maybe the barrier is that we already believe we are right - that we know the answer - that the other person is wrong. Once more, up come the barriers to effective listening. We are listening from our own frame of reference, at best we are only listening for the right to reply.

Mary understands the importance of listening - as Covey emphasises - seeking to understand the other person, before we try to be understood. She also knows that in certain circumstances, even listening attentively is not enough. For when we are listening attentively, we may be making a real effort, but we are still listening for the right to reply. As soon as the other person pauses, we will be into that gap like a rat up a drainpipe. We know the right answer and we cannot wait to give it.

That might be appropriate when the other person simply

requires information, but not when there is an emotional context to the conversation, or issues are really complex. Now, we really need to listen deeply for understanding, to cross the line, to get into the other person's frame of reference - to listen for the right to understand.

We achieve this when we move to a whole new level - when we empathically listen. Now we don't interrupt, we let pauses run on until the other person starts speaking again, we avoid asking questions as much possible, to prevent sending the other person off in a different direction, we do all we can, to understand how the other person is feeling.

I am convinced that if people were really willing to listen empathically - to listen deeply to understand the other person - difficult situations would make headway. The relationship with your partner that has fallen on difficult times, an issue at work brought to you by one of your team, a friend in need of advise, a complex disagreement with a supplier or customer.

When we listen for true understanding, we close our mouth and open not only our ears, but also our mind and our heart.

Somewhere out there, is someone who needs a damn good listening to, today.

## We should always seek better than compromise

Compromise may well be my least favourite word in the English language. I believe that all too often we are too quick to compromise.
I completely accept that compromise has made the world go round. It's what resolves differences, even intransigent

positions. It's how governments get legislation onto statute books, how management and union negotiations get resolved, how contract disputes are solved, how couples patch together tense relationships. It is so much better than conflict, or stalemate, or indeed, than win-lose outcomes. I am however, left with the feeling when we do compromise, we give something away; we accept second best, we move to a mid point.

If we are willing to search for it, we can always seek better than compromise. To do so really effectively, requires so many of those ideas we have explored as we have considered great relationships. It takes time, an open mind, creativity, a willingness to explore new options, even to accept that our original views may not have been right. Perhaps most importantly, it requires a win-win mentality and the determination to listen for understanding.

When we begin to engage with others in that process, it can be frustrating at first - really difficult. How much easier and quicker is it to rush to a compromise? If we stick at it, especially if both parties are willing to give it a go, over time, something magical takes place, new thinking emerges and we can arrive at an answer, a solution, that is even better than our starting position.

So, Mary will always try to seek better than compromise, no matter how tough it might seem. If we refuse to accept a simple compromise, but strive for better, so much more can be achieved.

Mary is both trusting and trustworthy. She works hard to build long-term, highly effective relationships. She knows that it is through great relationships, which demonstrate mutual benefit, that so much is achieved. Plus, it's so much easier to build those relationships with the right people on your bus.

# Case Study

Leaders exist at every level in organisations. A lot of my work is focussed at the top, supporting Chief Executives, Directors, Boards and Trustees, but I also take great pleasure in helping leaders develop everywhere.

There are a crucial group of leaders in any organisation, large and small. They are the people who sit below the senior team in the traditional hierarchy. Depending on the size of the organisation they are often heads of departments themselves, or what we often call middle managers, leading teams of their own.

Emphasis is too often only placed on the vertical responsibilities of these people, how they are performing in their role and the work of their teams. These are crucial people in any organisation - they are what I call the fulcrum - with key responsibilities both upwards and downwards. They are the communications hub of the organisation.

All too often, their focus is only vertical. They fail to communicate and work effectively with their peers and colleagues in different teams and departments across the organisation. When this occurs, we get what we call silo working, teams working in isolation to each other. When this happens and it is all too familiar, opportunities to co-operate and deliver mutual benefit are missed, teams become inward focussed and defensive, resources are not shared, people don't work towards joint objectives.

Those barriers can only be broken down, when these heads of department or middle managers begin to build relationships with each other, to understand they can develop a common purpose, to share resources, to work together interdependently.

I have recently been working with one such group of people in a large charity. My brief from 'on high' was to help them break down barriers and build relationships and co-operation between teams. The first few sessions were difficult. There was much mistrust and defensiveness, the legacy of a long period of silo working. I first had to convince this group of managers that they could become an effective horizontal team, as well as maintaining their important vertical responsibilities. It took time, a lot of effort, and a willingness to listen to one another, to realise they were on the same side, in the same organisation, with common goals - but slowly we got there.

We created a team charter, consisting of a clear purpose for why they exist as a team (not to be confused with their vertical responsibilities). We developed a framework for how they committed to behave together and decided how they would work together, including how often they would meet.

It has been far from plain sailing, old traditions die a slow death, but there has been real progress, which is bringing benefits for the whole organisation. An added bonus has been how much more effective this team now is at leading upwards, providing support for the senior team.

It really is all about relationships.

## Self reflection

Think of a relationship, inside or outside work where trust is high, and one where there is a lack of trust. Think through the differences between those relationships and the relative effectiveness of the results.

Consider in which relationships trust is currently low. Where do you need to build trust? How can you do so? What deposits could you make into the bank accounts of the other parties?

How effective are you at listening? Be really honest with yourself, are there occasions when you know you could listen better? Is this sometimes a barrier to true understanding? In which relationships or situations could you resolve to be a more effective listener?

## Further reading

'The Speed of Trust' by Stephen M R Covey

'The 7 Habits of Highly Effective People' by Stephen R Covey

# Notes

# Chapter EIGHT
## Right People on the Bus

'Get the right people on the bus, the wrong people off the bus, and the right people in the right seats'

Jim Collins

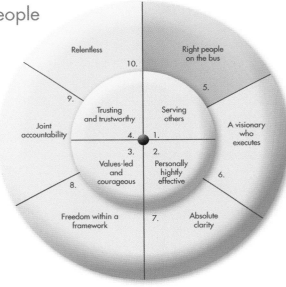

If the first four of Mary's traits lie deep in the inner circle - if they are about what defines her as a person - the remaining six traits are all about how Mary leads others. This often applies to the team she leads, but also to how she interacts with and gets the most out of, her boss, colleagues, external contacts, also her family, friends and immediate community. These are real people with whom Mary has a relationship, and remember, she already understands that it is through highly effective relationships that so much is achieved.

It is through being effective at leading others that Mary has a wider influence in the outer circle, where she leads in the organisation and beyond.

Mary's fifth trait as a leader is that she gets the right people on the bus (and the wrong people off.) I use the bus analogy so often that I do know it has become something of a cliché with my regular clients. They groan as we reference it again, but I also notice that it has become common language, not only when we are together, but often for them in their organisations. I find it such a powerful analogy and very easy to visualise. The principle is simply that If we want to take the bus on a journey, (delivering a vision, executing a project, getting things done as a team), we can only do so really successfully if we have the right people on our bus. This means we need a highly effective team, focussed on the goal, executing superbly, working together, supporting each other, and delivering every day. We need a team with the right blend of skills, the right attitude, at the front of the bus.

In the 'Good to Great' chapter 'First Who then What', Jim Collins also goes as far as to say get the right team on the bus, wrong people off the bus, before figuring out where to drive it.

This is all great in theory, as all this stuff is, but the reality is always far more complex. From time to time Mary will take on a new role, a new challenge and a new team. The reality is, as she gets to know them, she will realise they are in all sorts of seats on the bus. As she sits in the driving seat, there will be people next to her at the front of the bus, maybe even one or two wanting to help her drive. There will be a crowd of people in the middle of the bus, some trying their best, some not sure they are in the right seat, some trying to move forward, but a few idly gazing out of the window watching the world go by, imagining life on a different bus or on the golf course. Then there will be some towards the back of the bus. At best they are underperforming, have poor attitudes or both. At worst, they are what Mary recognises as being assassins, they are actively, sometimes even openly, trying to disrupt the journey - knock the bus off course, maybe even one or two are throwing nails out of the window trying to cause a puncture. Can you see it? It's a vivid picture and all too familiar.

Mary knows in this situation she has a lot of work to do and it will not happen overnight. She also knows that unless she faces up to the big challenges and takes the necessary action, in both the short and long term, she cannot be successful.

I work with many leaders who absolutely get the principle of right people on the bus. I can think of two in particular, I have had the privilege of supporting over the past few years as they strive to make it happen with their team. Just look at that last sentence again, 'over the past few years' ...for this takes time and in reality, it never stops.

Both these leaders arrived to take the top job in their organisations. They were brought in to deliver a turnaround in the fortunes, to make the breakthrough from good to great. Both inherited an already existing senior team and both knew within weeks, that significant changes were necessary. These were not, on the whole, bad people in the team, they were just not the right people to take the organisation forward. Some were part of the problem, not the solution. Tackling these issues is never easy, dealing with real people and real emotions, but these two leaders knew it was the right thing to do. As both display so many of Mary's characteristics, both were determined to do that right thing, in the right way.

For Mary, this means being determined and relentless, but always fair. This is where her values-led trait comes to the fore. It means tackling issues, not ignoring them, it means not jumping to conclusions, taking the time to ensure you are right, but then having the difficult conversations earlier rather than later. Treating every person with respect and as an individual.

Through this approach, both leaders made substantial progress over their first year or so in the role. They changed every member of their senior team, but in different ways. Some had to be removed from the bus, some chose to get off at an appropriate bus stop and move to new challenges (one grabbed the life changing opportunity to move abroad for a new start for their family) and some were changed through the inspiration and support of these leaders. The teams grew under their new leaders and are still there today, now at the front of the bus making a positive contribution to the journey. There are many different ways in which to change people.

Mary also recognises that in any team, it is not just the results her people deliver that matter, it is also their attitude.

This is a really significant change of emphasis from that which so often exists in organisations. Traditionally, we have measured people by how capable they are, by the results they deliver. There is a second imperative however - people also behave in the right way. When this breakthrough in thinking occurs, it can result in a radically different approach to how we recruit, lead and develop our people.

Mary plots this by using the very simple matrix. The vertical axis represents how effective they are in their current role - the results they are delivering. The horizontal axis is about their behaviours and attitude.

Each axis is numbered 0-10. Using her understanding of each individual person, based on a combination of evidence and intuition, she can then place each of her people on the matrix using this scoring system.

For example, a person delivering steady, if unspectacular, results but who has a great attitude which has a positive impact on the rest of the team, might score 6 on the vertical axis and 8 on the horizontal axis. Conversely, someone who delivers good results consistently, but who has a poor attitude which can spread negative energy might be an 8 and a 2. You could do this for your team now. Be as honest as you can in your scoring. You may well end up with a matrix with people dotted in many different places as in the illustration.

You can now divide the matrix into four quadrants by drawing vertical and horizontal lines along the number 5. People in each quadrant present different challenges. Those in the top right quadrant are up there with you on the journey - they are potential drivers and need nurturing and developing to unlock their potential. The problem is, too often we ignore these people because we are dealing with issues elsewhere. We ignore them at our peril because if we do so, at best we are failing to unleash their full potential, at worse we leave ourselves open to them being poached by other organisations.

Those in the bottom right quadrant, above average in attitude but below average in capability and results, need individual action plans to build their capability. Those in the bottom left need individual plans too, but here, significant improvement in both areas is necessary if they are to remain on the bus.

It is those top left quadrant people who present the biggest challenge, delivering results for you but with a below average, often poor attitude. When I present this material, I get lots of knowing nods. Most of us have those people in our teams and organisations. They are often long servers. All too often we ignore the issues, because 'it's only Fred, he's always been like that', but every day they are draining energy form those around them.

Mary understands you cannot ignore behaviour and attitude issues - they will not go away. She knows they are not easy to tackle, particularly if they have been ignored for years, but she will address them, always with determination, always fairly, and always treating everyone as an individual.

Where organisations do accept that how someone behaves is as equally important as the results they deliver, it can lead to a transformational change in the way people are recruited and managed and can be built into recruitment and performance management systems.

So how does Mary go about ensuring she has the right people on the bus? Through a rigorous approach to

# Capability and
# Attitude Matrix

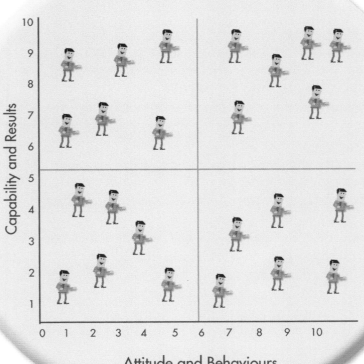

recruitment, development and where necessary, to people leaving the bus.

We all know how difficult it is to ensure successful recruitment. Every one of us (certainly including Mary and me) has made a wrong recruitment decision in the past. We know that when we do make that wrong decision, it can often take a long, long time and much pain to resolve the issue. Doing all we can to reduce the chances of making the wrong decision to start with is therefore essential.

As ever, it comes down to the amount of time and rigour that we put into recruitment. Mary understands this and ensures she allocates sufficient time to this crucial task. She understands that relying on an interview alone is never enough. It's always possible to blag an interview! So, she also ensures she uses a combination of other options, depending on the role, to support the interview. These may include where appropriate, presentations, psychometric testing and ensuring candidates spend time with her people, as part of the process.

Involving others informally in the recruitment process can be invaluable. Get candidates to spend time with some of the team they are going to be working with. Then seek the views of the team. Often candidates will behave very differently in a more relaxed environment than they will in the formal interview. This can be one factor that influences your decision - in either direction. Even your receptionist will have a valuable contribution to make, having observed behaviours before the interview – there will be very little missed!

This still does not guarantee Mary always makes the right decisions but it reduces the risk. She is rigorous in pursuing references, often contacting a variety of people to seek their views, rather than relying on a standard written reference. Mary also uses probationary periods as exactly that.

If you genuinely agree that how someone behaves in their role, is as important as the results they deliver, do all you can to make sure you include ways of covering this in the recruitment process. If you can recruit people who have a values-fit with the organisation, the chances of them being truly effective in the role will significantly increase.

Finally, Mary also strongly believes in one of Jim Collins' key findings, 'when in doubt don't hire, keep looking.' This can be very hard to follow, especially when a post needs filling urgently, but she knows that too often when we recruit in haste, we repent at leisure. If in doubt, don't recruit. As a client of mine once sagely remarked, 'it's better to have a hole than an a*** hole!'

Getting the right people on the bus is not all about recruitment. One of the most satisfying ways we can do this is when we develop our people, when we succeed on moving them forward on the bus. Mary ensures she devotes sufficient time to developing her people. This happens in a variety of ways, because every one is an individual. It all begins with understanding every single person - what makes them tick - what their specific needs are. This comes through taking the time to listen. Mary tailors a plan specifically for them, whether it's around training, formal courses, learning new skills, being given stretching opportunities, having a career plan in place, study, or through coaching. The secret is about treating every person as a unique individual.

Just sometimes though, people need to leave the bus. No amount of development is going to alter the situation. For whatever reason, they are simply the wrong person for the bus. This does not necessarily make them a bad person, they may simply be on the wrong bus. Recognising this may be the first step to them leaving at the next stop and finding the right bus for them.

I have many examples of this happening. It has proved to be the best thing that could possibly happen to that individual, no matter how painful it is at the time. Equally, that person may be on the right bus, but in the wrong seat. A change of role, or department, may be the answer. Never use this as an excuse for handing on a people problem. Mary's values would never allow her to do that.

As we learn from 'Good to Great', 'when you know you need to make a people change, act...'
Never ignore these issues in the hope they will go away, because they won't. If someone has to leave the bus, do it quickly and fairly. Do the right thing in the right way. You will gain enormous respect if people see you act in the right way, rather than ignoring issues.

There's a really important point to emphasise here. If we ignore our problem people, if we allow poor performance and poor behaviours to go unchecked, if we fail to deal with people issues, our good people will notice. They will become resentful that the others are able to get away with it. It might even lead them to look for a 'better' organisation to work with. Conversely, if we act fairly and decisively, it can have really positive impact on our good people.

Mary works hard to ensure she leads a balanced team, where her people have a range of complimentary strengths. She does not look to recruit in her type, and knows that in a team, she needs people with big ideas, but also people who get on and execute. She needs people who will constructively challenge her and suggest better ways of doing things.

There are many models out there for building balanced teams. I do love the 'Strengths Finder 'material. An online analysis tool allows you to understand your primary strengths and those of your team. It can be used to assist with recruitment, development and building the most effective team with complementary skills. It's well worth a look and is based on the proposition that we should understand and play to a person's strengths, rather than constantly trying to mitigate their weaknesses.

Remember also, there are many leaders out there who are, and who aspire to be Mary, who do not even lead teams. They will be in roles that do not involve line managing others. All the principles we have explored in this trait still apply, but often in the context of working effectively with others in project teams, with volunteers, with people from other departments. Ensuring you have the right people on the bus is as essential for a temporary project team as it is for a long-term management team. Mary may have less control over creating that team, but that does not make the principle any less important.

I love this definition of leadership I came across

'Surround yourself with the right people then just grind it out.'

It's all about getting the right people on your bus.

So, hopefully a lot to think about there! Getting the right people on the bus, and the wrong people off, is an essential trait of a highly effective leader. So is someone who dreams big dreams but also delivers.

# Case Study

There is a commonly held misconception that anyone who is a 'people person' is a soft manager. This is a myth perpetuated by 'Bills' everywhere. It's simply not true. It's completely possible to care about your people, to want to do the best for them, but also to take the tough decisions and to act decisively, whenever it is necessary.

Back in my corporate world 'people persons' were few and far between, but there were notable exceptions. One was a young leader - one of my few role models and inspirations, back then. She stood out even then, because of her commitment to her people. She has since gone on to a very successful career, leading the UK division of an international restaurant brand.

Recently she was named the Most People-Focused CEO in the private sector at the HR Excellence Awards. She inherited a brand that was 'tired, dated and on the way out', where 'the love had gone and people had lost pride'. Over the last few years a remarkable transformation has taken place within the brand, based around four principles:

**Recognition is key to success:** she introduced recognition and reward schemes. She rewards staff who have impressed during mystery customer visits. Last year she flew 400 of her people to Florida for a party. 'We can't afford not to do it', she says, 'it's a huge deposit in the emotional bank account.'

**Don't be afraid to lose people:** this is where we can destroy the myth that there is anything soft about being a 'people person.' It's about taking tough decisions, implementing them fairly and in the right way. This leader knows that her business can only be successful if she has the right people on the bus. This can only ever involve the wrong people leaving the bus.

She assessed everyone (yes, everyone) in her organisation and classified them as 'players', 'winnable players', 'potential players' and 'assassins.' Out went the assassins, in the first year, 12% of the 3,000 employees.

**Get on top of succession planning:** she seeks to groom successors internally, at every level. 70% of unit managers are now internal appointments. No one is appointed as a general manager directly from outside the company. This ensures people really do understand the culture and values.

**Be authentic:** it is no surprise to learn that she has placed values right at the heart of the business. Pride, passion and personality. 'You have to be authentic, brands have to have an emotional attachment. If it's real you'll feel it.'

## Self reflection

Do the 'Capability and Attitude Matrix' for your team. Be as honest and objective as you can be. If trust is high enough, individually discuss your analysis with your team, comparing your positioning of them on the matrix with their views. Create individual action plans for each person.

Think back to a disastrous recruitment decision you made or were involved in. We all have them! Analyse what could have been done better. Consider what additional recruitment tools you could use to support the interview process.

Have you got the right people on your bus? Are they in the right seats? Is there a 'people' decision you have been putting off? What should you do about it? Today!

## Further reading

'First Who Then What' chapter from 'Good to Great' by Jim Collins

'Strengths Finder 2.0' by Tom Rath

# Notes

# Chapter NINE
## A Visionary Who Executes

'Vision without action is
merely a dream.
Action without
vision just passes
the time.
Vision with
action can
change the
world'

Joel A Barker

Relentless

Right people
on the bus

10.

9.

5.

Trusting
and trustworthy

Serving
others

Joint
accountability

A visionary
who
executes

4. 1.

3. 2.

Values-led
and
courageous

Personally
highly
effective

6.

8.

Freedom within a
framework

7.

Absolute
clarity

I thought long and hard before putting vision and execution into the same trait. At first they might seem like very opposing skills, but I am convinced they are entirely complementary, indeed the mix of both is an essential characteristic of great leaders.

Let's begin with two more quotes. The first is from Jack Welch, former head of the giant GE corporation, He said:

'Great leaders create a vision, articulate the vision, communicate the vision, and relentlessly drive it to completion.'

Then we come to Bill Gates, founder of Microsoft and today possibly the world's best known philanthropist, who said:

'Vision without execution is daydreaming.'

In other words, if you put the two together, great leaders must be visionary, but they must also understand that executing, getting the job done, is absolutely essential as well.

It's a theme taken up by Jim Collins in his latest book 'Great by Choice.' He talks about how highly effective leaders possess and practice the ability to both 'zoom in' and zoom out.' I believe this is a brilliant description of vision and execution. When we zoom out as leaders we take a step back, we focus on the bigger picture, we look around us, we look ahead, we horizon scan. When we zoom in, we focus on the detail of a particular task or issue, we get the job done, in other words we execute, or ensure execution by others. I think leadership is about constantly zooming out and zooming in, allocating sufficient time and resources to each, knowing when it is appropriate to focus on each of those separate but entirely complementary activities.

Incidentally, whenever I have introduced this concept to clients I am working with, it has been universally well received (as another massive dose of common sense) and several leaders have begun to allocate specific meetings to these two activities, with 'zoom in and zoom out time' becoming part of their organisation or team's common language.

So, why do you need to possess both skills?
Firstly, I think if you don't do either well, you cannot be successful as a leader. Maybe that is obvious. Leaders

need to be visionary, to look ahead, to create a picture of the future and then to sell it to those who want to contribute to the journey. To echo Bill Gates, on its own that is not enough. Unless you ensure the job gets done, the project delivered, the strategy achieved, the vision realised, you cannot be effective.

There is some debate as to whether a great leader needs to execute themselves. No pun intended... you know what I mean! That's not really the point for me. It may be that Mary is at the top of a large organisation, in which case she will have multi layers of people reporting to her. In this instance, much of the execution will be delegated, but her essential role is to make sure it happens, to have the structures, checks, balances and measures in place to ensure it happens. Remember, 'Marys' can exist everywhere in organisations - she may have a front line role with no team of her own. This makes her role as a leader no less important, but means she is unlikely to have anyone to delegate execution to, so will therefore get on with it herself.

Equally, both 'Marys' will be visioning at different levels. One might focus on organisational strategy and the other on a local project or initiative, but both still have the necessity to paint a picture of the future, to envisage and share an end in mind with others and to communicate it brilliantly, if they are to be effective.

So, let's look first at Mary's role in visioning. For me, this is no more than painting a picture of a desired point in the future, in a way that engages others to join the journey. Great leaders at every level do this. They understand that unless people have a picture of where the bus is going, they are unlikely to want to be in the front seats and even less likely to fully contribute to the journey. It's also about feeling work is important and worthwhile. We are much more likely to feel engaged, if we can see our contribution is helping the team or organisation get to a better place. Incidentally, a great way for a team of people to develop a picture of the future together is to draw it - literally. I have spent many hours with teams and giant pieces of paper, encouraging them to create their pictures. Drawing releases innovative thinking and creativity in a way words simply cannot. Of course, once the picture is complete, it can then be put into words to enable it to be articulated and communicated, but remember that famous saying, 'a picture is worth a thousand words'.

A vision is really a picture of the outcome of something you want to change. So much of what Mary does as a great leader, is to deliver change. It's what leaders do all the time, for organisational success is about constant change. If we don't change we get left behind and eventually we become irrelevant and extinct. As Charles Darwin said

'It's not the strongest of the species that survive, nor the most intelligent, but the ones most adaptable to change.'

Change can be extremely daunting for those required to deliver it and scary and uncomfortable for those who are faced by it. Change is unsettling and few people enjoy it. Which is a great pity, because it is through changing that we develop, remain relevant and fit for purpose.

Back in my corporate days, I was given a series of promotions into new roles. Each time my new boss would tell me that I needed to change things, to make things better, to deliver improved results. I found this really daunting - where should I begin? Over the years however, I learned of two change models which I now use and teach as frameworks for delivering successful change.

The first is an eight-step change process by John Kotter from the book 'Leading Change.' That's the academic text, but he has also written a fable, to demonstrate the eight steps in (for me) a more pleasing form. Titled 'Our Iceberg is Melting', it tells the story through the eyes of a colony of penguins in Antarctica, facing the challenge of their iceberg home melting. Get hold of the book if you can - it's a simple and engaging read, with lots of pictures of cute penguins... that really worked for me!

In summary, Kotter's eight stage process looks like this:

1. Reduce complacency and increase urgency

2. Pull a team together to guide the needed change

3. Create a vision and strategy

4. Communicate the vision and strategy (by capturing hearts and minds, not through 144 power point slides!) Build understanding and buy-in.

5. Empower others to act, removing barriers so those who want to make the vision a reality can do so

6. Create some short-term wins

7. Don't let up, be relentless until the vision is a reality

8. Make the changes stick, because tradition dies a hard death

One of the many things I love about this model is, creating the vision is only the third step in the chain. It is preceded by the need to create a sense of urgency and put together the right team to deliver the change. Mary completely understands the necessity of both of these first steps. If people have an insufficient sense of urgency they will not buy into change and without the right team around her she cannot hope to make the change happen (or to execute it, in other words)

The other framework I often use is called 'The Circle of Organisational Effectiveness', still the most powerful tool I know for diagnosing what needs to change, then delivering that change in any team, project or organisation.

In summary, the model recognises if we are to build an effective team or organisation, it must focus on delivering what stakeholders want and need, or at least building enough understanding of those wants and needs to inform decision making. Then, great teams and organisations align what they do to those stakeholder wants and needs. Through those actions, they build an overall direction of travel (a purpose, values and vision), a route to get there (a strategy), aligned resources (right people, structures, systems, processes etc.) and the right culture. They constantly work to ensure each of these are in place and effective (because change is constant).

Mary understands that part of being a visionary leader is about ensuring her team or organisation is absolutely clear on why they exist, what their purpose is. She takes the time to review that purpose from time to time, to ensure it is still relevant. The 'Hedgehog Concept' in 'Good to Great' gives an excellent model for reviewing purpose. Collins and his team set out how great organisations have an absolutely clear understanding of their purpose, which consists of three elements; what we are deeply passionate about, what we can be best in the world at and what our key measure of economic success is. Have a look at the chapter in 'Good to Great' to learn more.

Mary understands that as a leader, she constantly needs to ensure she is communicating effectively. She does this in a variety of ways, right round the 360 degrees of the middle circle from the inside-out leadership model we looked at, right back at the beginning of the book. With her team, she communicates informally at every opportunity, even if it's a quick chat by the coffee machine, in 1-1s, and in team meetings.

If Mary happens to be at the head of an organisation or leading a large team, she also holds regular communications events. Maybe twice a year, or even quarterly, she brings her people together, takes the opportunity to reflect on progress, re-enforce the vision, celebrate success and seek feedback. If she leads many people, there may be several sessions, maybe at differing locations. These events take time and commitment but Mary knows effective on-going communication is essential.

Alongside being a visionary Mary also possesses the ability to 'zoom in' whenever necessary, to get the job done, to execute, or depending on her role, to ensure execution. She does this by ensuring her vision is broken down into a strategy, into operational plans and ultimately into individual work plans. She ensures every person has absolute clarity on what is expected of him or her and they have the support and tools to enable them to deliver. We will examine this further in the next chapter, as we explore Mary's leadership trait of providing absolute clarity.

Like any great leader, Mary recognises that she must find time to think. Leaders at all levels have hectic schedules. Increasingly in this modern world of work we are busy, our diaries are filled with meetings, there is a constant barrage of emails and other demands on our time. If we don't take time out to think, how can we ever move forward, keep ourselves fresh, dream and plan the future, ensure continual improvement? Mary has as full a schedule as everyone else, but she absolutely disciplines herself to build in thinking time. Sometimes, she gets out of the office and goes for a walk. It clears her head and gives her the space she needs to think.

She also ensures her team are encouraged to take time to do so. She champions the need for creativity in her people - how can you be creative without the time to think? It's a great example of what we mean by 'zooming out'.

Mary possess the ability to make even complex strategies really simple, when it comes to putting plans in place, communicating the various steps and making it happen. She is also assiduous in her measurement of progress, another trait we will return to in a later chapter.

The more I study leadership, and observe great leaders in action, the more I see the ability they have, to be both visionary and to execute highly effectively. It's no more complicated than doing the right things right. Simple really, not rocket science, but great leadership is based on simple principles.

But you can't hope to execute effectively unless your people are absolutely clear on what you want them to deliver.

# Case Study

The most inspiring leaders I work with are those who possess that ability to paint a clear and compelling picture of the future, in a way that engages me and makes me want to be part of the journey. It's an ability great leaders just seem to have.

Let me tell you about one in particular whom I have had the privilege to work with.

We return to my corporate days and to one of the few leaders who genuinely inspired me. This was in the early days of the development of high street leisure brands. This leader was responsible for the development of two of the best known of those brands, both of which are still very much at the forefront today, having enjoyed long-term success.

This was new territory for many of us involved with the developments, but her ability to paint a picture of the future was immense, not just in describing the physical attributes of the brands, but much more importantly, how they would feel. It's at this level that you gain emotional commitment from your followers.

Not only did she have the ability to create a compelling vision, she was also highly skilled at executing. She ensured she had the right people on the bus and every single one of them knew exactly what was expected of them. Major development and roll-out projects were driven forward with absolute clarity, targets, milestones and measures.

Remember, vision without execution is daydreaming.

## Self reflection

Have you set out a clear and compelling vision for your team or organisation? Do you communicate it clearly and regularly?

Think of a change project or initiative you have been involved in, or are currently planning. Consider it in the light of Kotter's 8 step change process. How could you use that framework to increase the chances of successful and sustainable change?

How effective are you at ensuring execution? Do you spend enough time as a leader ensuring that plans are translated into action? How can you ensure you 'zoom in' when necessary, to clear road blocks, provide clarity and focus, and ensure effective execution?

## Further reading

'Leading Change' by John Kotter

'Our Iceberg is Melting' by John Kotter

'The Four Disciplines of Execution'
by Chris McChesney et al

The Hedgehog Concept chapter
from 'Good to Great' by Jim Collins

'Great by Choice' by Jim Collins

# Notes

# Chapter TEN
## Absolute Clarity

'Without clear goals
we become
strangely
obsessed with
daily acts of
trivia'

Anon.

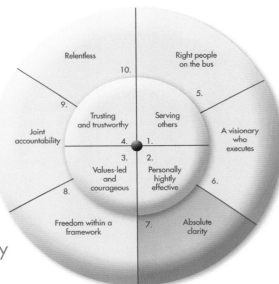

'Complexity is
your enemy. Any
fool can make
things complicated.
It's hard to keep
things simple'

Richard Branson

Another of Mary's great strengths is she provides people
with absolute clarity. As we examine this trait, I will
primarily focus on Mary's role in providing her own team
with absolute clarity, but remember this applies to anyone
she comes into contact with.

But let's begin by introducing a simple model for getting things done, called the 'Execution Model'. What do we want from our people? Well, we want them to deliver great results for us, every single day. That's why we employ them. In order to deliver those great results day in day out, we need our people to execute superbly and consistently, to get the job done right. No rocket science so far. In order for people to execute superbly, two factors must be in place.

Firstly our people need clarity - they need to know what we want of them and how to do it. Without absolute clarity how can people execute effectively? Clarity on its own is not enough - they also need to be engaged, which is the 'want to do'.

If neither is in place, how could people possibly get the job done? If however, they know what to do, but don't want to do it, they will not be truly effective. Equally, if they are the most enthusiastic people in the world, highly engaged, full of 'want to do', but do not know what is expected of them, they cannot execute effectively.

Who provides that clarity and engagement? Highly effective leaders at every level, who first ensure they have the right people on their bus.

We will return to building engagement in the next chapter, but for now let's examine this trait of providing people with absolute clarity.

Mary really does understand that people work best when they do have clarity. She seeks to do that at two different levels.

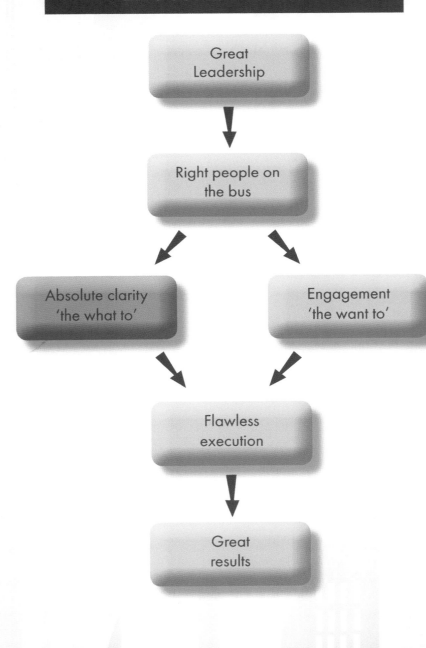

Firstly, she tries to ensure her people understand how what they are doing, fits into the bigger picture. This is called 'line of sight'. She knows if she can provide that line of sight, it will ensure people realise their role is relevant, important and they are contributing to the overall purpose and direction of their team - ultimately, their whole organisation.

It is possible to provide this line of sight for every role, no matter how junior in our hierarchical structures, no matter how many layers there are in the organisation. It is completely possible to give each person clarity over the purpose, values, vision and strategy of the whole organisation. Of course, this needs to be proportionate - someone in a demanding front line job does not need a three hour weekly briefing on organisational strategy, but the skill of leadership is to establish line of sight at just the right level.

Mary does this in one to one sessions, but also by organising communications events and briefings, inviting senior leaders and colleagues from across the organisation to meet and brief her people. She makes absolutely sure her team members understand how they help to deliver her goals and objectives, and those of the team as a whole.

Secondly, Mary ensures that every individual team member has absolute clarity of their own role, and what they are there to deliver. She does this through a piece of material called 'The Power of 3.'

She first ensures clarity of role - why any job exists. This is done by creating a role statement for each job, which never exceeds 20 words. This sounds really simple, but often is not so. When I ask groups of people to write their succinct role statements, their first reaction is that it is too simple a task. After five minutes or so of contemplation, I see many furrowed brows and much chewing of pens. Many people find it genuinely hard to record what their job is about, because in our working world of over-complexity, we have too often lost sight of the basics.

Mary then makes sure that at any one time, her people are focussed on delivering only a limited number of goals. So often I come across people with dozens of goals and objectives. When I ask them which of these have priority I am frequently told that they all do. In this situation, no-one can be truly effective. Indeed, there is ample evidence that if we are focussed on say, ten things at any one time, the chances of delivering any of them with excellence is nil. Even with five things we may struggle to deliver more than one or two of them with excellence. When we are only focussed on our three highest priorities at any one time, the chances of delivering all three with excellence, dramatically increases.

How is this possible? How, in our modern, complex world of work could we possibly be focussed on just three things? This is the breakthrough point. We have made our working world complex, but never confuse complexity, or resulting busyness, with effectiveness. They are very different things.

How does Mary enable her people to focus on just three highest priorities at any one time? By setting a few 'Power of 3' ground rules, as follows:

1. The three goals should account for around 70% of activity in any given week. In other words 70% of a person's time should be focussed on delivering those three goals. Much more than 70% is unrealistic - there is always other stuff to do. Much less than 70%

suggests these three are not the most truly important things.

2. The trick is to get them at just the right level. Too broad and they lack focus and clarity, too detailed and it is unlikely there will be only three.

3. Each goal will contain detail below it of how to make it happen, how to execute the goal. Of course the devil is in the detail, but at this level they cannot contain every piece of it.

4. Each goal must be measurable and regularly reviewed and measured.

5. In some roles, goals will be long-term and the focus will be on breaking them down into manageable chunks. In other roles the goals may actually change regularly.

Mary understands that her role is to enable her people to deliver their goals. She ensures they have the clarity but are then given sufficient freedom to deliver. She holds regular reviews to monitor progress, and support delivery. Here, we see so many other traits in action including serving others, freedom within a framework and joint accountability. As we work our way through Mary's traits I am hoping you are beginning to see the interdependencies between them. They are everywhere.

When this works effectively, it can make monitoring someone's performance so easy. It provides real focus for regular 1-1s (they can primarily focus on the 'Power of 3'), but also can be built simply and elegantly into performance management systems and appraisals.

I cannot stress too highly how crucial it is for leaders to hold regular 1-1s with their people. I think there is no more important a session. Too often, I come across managers who have the best of intentions for holding these sessions but all too frequently cancel them, because other urgent things get in the way.
Always urgent things - often not important things.

Another barrier I hear frequently is managers are too busy to have time to hold regular 1-1s. I accept people are really busy these days - it's a word I hear time and time again, but never confuse busy-ness with effectiveness. They are very different things. Indeed, this busy-ness is often a result of not having regular 1-1s.

I am often told that a manager has too many direct reports to be able to hold 1-1s. If they have ten or more direct reports, I agree with them. The problem here is not the 1-1s, it's the number of direct reports and although it might be tough to find solutions, it's the structure which needs addressing.

Doubters also say they are not necessary because they see their people informally on a daily basis. That's great and long may it continue - informal catch-ups are important, but never let them detract from holding a regular formal session.

I understand it's more challenging if your team is based remotely. So make it happen - virtually if necessary, although face to face contact is also still very important when possible.

The frequency and duration of 1-1s will vary according to need, but as a guide I believe once a month for an hour is about right. They should also be personalised to the needs of the individual, but can follow a simple basic agenda:

- How has the team member performed against their 'Power of 3' goals since the last 1-1?

- What are the areas of focus before the next 1-1?

- What does the leader need to do to enable the team member to successfully deliver?

Top and tail the session with a personal catch up (for which you need a genuine desire to get to know the whole person) and you have the perfect 1-1 framework.

There are lots of places it's possible to hold 1-1s, often it's really good to get out of the office. Holding a 1-1 in the office may be most time efficient, but a change of environment can really work very well.

Mary particularly understands the power of walking and talking, not only occasionally for 1-1s, but if she has a particular issue she wants to address. She doesn't restrict this to members of her team, she also takes a stroll sometimes with clients, and other business contacts. Getting out in the fresh air and ensuring she listens effectively, can be a great way to explore and resolve even the most complex or intransigent of issues.

It's something Steve Jobs was famous for. In Walter Isaacson's excellent biography, he explains how Jobs would frequently walk and talk with business associates and colleagues. It was the way he resolved the most difficult of issues and shaped his business deals.

There's even that moment near the end of that wonderful film 'The Queen', when the monarch expresses her hope *that Prime Minister Tony Blair is a walker, before leading him and the corgis through the grounds of Buckingham Palace!*

*1-1s are just one part of great performance management. They provide an opportunity, on a regular basis, to review performance, but are supplemented by frequent informal contact, and by some kind of annual appraisal process.*

*A word on appraisals. Many organisations have these processes in place but they will never be effective if a process is all they remain. At worst, they become an excruciating annual meeting, which neither boss nor team member wants to be at with the most uncomfortable of conversations resulting. Where they work best, they simply provide formal documentation, to support a robust approach to performance management on a continual basis, which is deeply embedded in the organisation's culture. Ensuring great performance management is the responsibility of every leader, not just the domain of HR.*

Mary puts considerable time and effort into providing clarity and reviewing progress. She knows when people have that clarity, they are half way towards effective execution.

A final thought on complexity, linked to Richard Branson's quote at the start of this chapter. Complexity really is our enemy. It is everywhere and frankly some people delight in it, because it provides wonderful excuses for not being held accountable. The skill great leaders like Mary possess, is they can see through complexity and from it they create simplicity. From simplicity comes clarity.

To quote Terry Leahy:

'change in any fast-moving, fast growing company is not easy. My solution is quite simple: to make things simple.
Simplicity is the knife that cuts through the tangled spaghetti of life's problems.'

The 'Power of 3' is a powerful tool to deliver that clarity and simplicity. Clarity on its own is not enough. Our people also must be engaged.

# Case Study

I work with a leader who totally gets the value of providing absolute clarity and has introduced it throughout her team and organisation.

When she took over as Chief Executive, she first took the time to define the roles of her senior team. In turn, she asked them to do exactly the same with their teams and so on, right through the hierarchy to the front line. If this sounds like a simple exercise, it wasn't. It led to many debates and much soul searching, particularly as people began to question the validity and relevance of certain roles. It led to realignment of roles, and some restructuring, but it was absolutely necessary as a start point, in building a highly effective organisation.

From this exercise, emerged the real line of sight. People could now see why their roles were important and a direct link through to the purpose, vision and strategy of the whole organisation. Their sense of personal worth increased. This leader even produced simple summary role statements for everyone, onto one (very large) organisational structure chart. The effect was immense, for now people saw interdependencies across the organisation, leading to the breaking down of silos and increased co-operation.

She then commenced a process of developing 'Power of 3' goals for everyone, introducing the concept and framework one level at a time, down through the organisation. She also insisted on regular 1-1s everywhere, understanding that she and her team needed to role model this way of working consistently.

It has taken time and there has been a need to constantly revisit and re-energise, but the impact has been to build a highly focused and effective organisation based on the principles of clarity and simplicity.

## Self reflection

How clear are you on your job role and your 'Power of 3' goals? Take time to reflect on them and write them down. How much time do you really spend on your most important goals in a typical week?

How clear are your team on their roles and goals? Could you spend time with each of them, revisiting and ensuring you are providing them with absolute clarity?

What barriers are preventing your team members

from being even more effective at executing on their most important goals? What role can you play, to help identify and remove those barriers?

# Further reading

'The Four Disciplines of Execution'
by Chris McChesney et al

# Notes

# Chapter ELEVEN
## Freedom Within a Framework

'Liberty, when it begins to take root, is a plant of rapid growth.'

George Washington

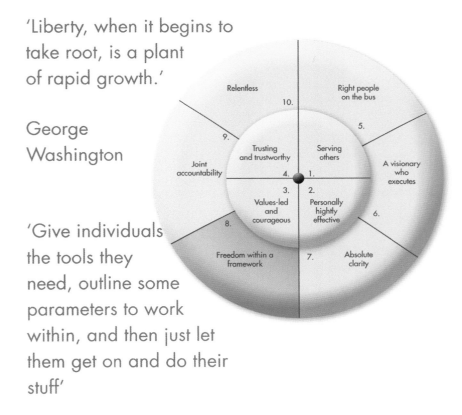

'Give individuals the tools they need, outline some parameters to work within, and then just let them get on and do their stuff'

Richard Branson

In this chapter we explore Mary's eighth trait as a highly effective leader, that she gives people freedom within a framework, and encourages creative discipline.

Our starting point is to return to the execution model introduced in the last chapter, when we looked at Mary's trait of giving people absolute clarity. You may remember, for people to execute effectively and deliver consistently great results, they must have that clarity, they must understand what to do and how to do it. This is only half of what is required - they must also be engaged and want to do it. It is only when we fully engage our people that we can expect to get the most from them.

There are many ways to engage people, as we will explore later, but a fundamental element is that we must give our people just the right amount of freedom to get on with their jobs. Too little freedom and we smother them, too much and we are in danger of abandoning them, of allowing things to slip out of control. In other words, we must empower them.

My problem with the concept of empowerment - it's another one of these awful management buzzwords you see being bandied about in text books. For ages I struggled to come up with a simple, meaningful definition of empowerment, until I came across the concept of 'freedom within a framework.'

I first saw this term coined in 'Good to Great' by Jim Collins. It's within a very underrated (in my view) chapter called 'A Culture of Discipline'. It summarises the finding of Collins and his research team.

In the highly effective organisations they studied, a common finding was, they seemed to be full of people with freedom to be creative in getting their job done, but within a highly disciplined framework. Where that disciplined framework was part of the culture, managers did not need to spend time imposing that discipline, people did it themselves, by being creative, but focussing that creativity only on their most important goals. It's the idea that hand in hand with

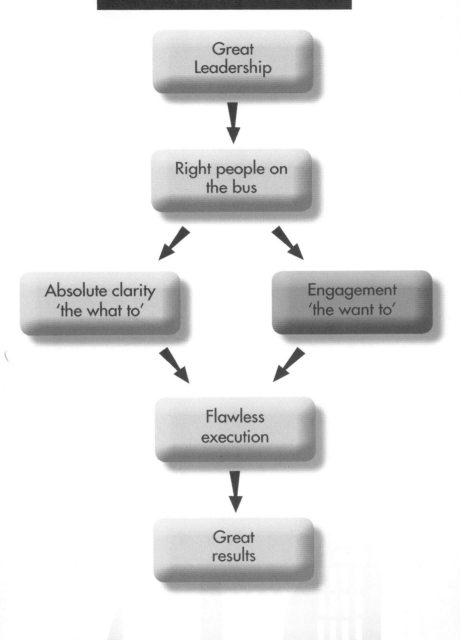

freedom comes responsibility and accountability. These traits really are starting to join up now.

Mary believes that people perform at their best when they are given freedom without unnecessary checking up and supervision. She also understands that giving people just the right level of freedom is crucial, but she always strives to give as much as she can. She notices that many people she works with revel in that freedom and produce great results. She encourages her people to work creatively, but only and always on the right things.

Empowerment does sound like a complex theory, but in reality it's really straightforward. In simple terms, it is just about giving your people freedom within a framework. There are many levels of empowerment - like so many other things, there is a continuum of empowerment, from very low freedom to very high levels.

When introducing people to this concept, I liken it to growing tomatoes... stick with this! When we grow tomatoes we first need to put the right conditions in place to allow the plants to flourish. We find just the right spot in which to grow them, we purchase the grow bags and the seedlings or young plants.

We plant them and look after them carefully in the early days. We ensure they have sufficient sunlight. We water them daily. We support them with canes and in time, the plants begin to grow. Now we check on their progress regularly, watering them when necessary.

We are there when needed - we do not abandon them. If we did, they would wither and die. Over time, the plants grow strong, they flourish, and eventually, with enough love and care, the tomatoes themselves grow, and we can harvest the fruit of our labours.

If that all sounds contrived I'm sorry, but I love it! I also think 'growing tomatoes' is the perfect description of what empowerment is all about. If we first look after our people carefully, ensure they are ready to take more responsibility, then step back, let them grow, but support them as needed, (but not with canes necessarily!) and never abandon them, we too can enjoy the fruits of their endeavours.

Empowerment is no more complex than that. Let's return to our continuum and consider various levels of empowerment. At one end of the continuum would be very low levels of empowerment. At this end we would give someone clear instructions, with little room for manoeuvre and then closely supervise them as they complete the task. In certain circumstances, such as, if the person is new and inexperienced, or the task complex or risky, this would be entirely appropriate. At the other end of the continuum would be a very high level of empowerment, where we set out what needs doing, then step right back, giving a large amount of freedom for someone to complete the task. Even at this end, we never abandon them, we are available to step in and support or redirect, but only when needed. As we move along the continuum, the level of empowerment grows. The appropriate place on the continuum is entirely dictated by a mixture of risk and confidence depending on the task and the person, but as a general rule we should look to give as much freedom as we can, to increase empowerment, but only ever within a framework. Failure to provide the framework risks abandonment.

As the song goes... 'there are three steps to heaven', or in this case, just three steps to successful empowerment!
Step one is to provide the framework, by giving absolute clarity on the task, agreeing a clear end in mind and setting out what tools and resources will be available to complete the task.
Step two is then to step back, to give the freedom, to enable the person to get on with the task.
Step three is to provide just the right level of support, whether it's a daily check-in, a weekly phone call, a monthly report, every instance is different, but the principles remain the same.

Mary works hard to maximise the level of freedom she gives her people, without ever abandoning them. She doesn't always get it right (remember Mary always strives to do the right thing but is far from perfect.) She understands there are many barriers to empowering, both from the person taking on the task, but also from the person setting the task. How often do we think it would be so much easier just to do the job ourselves? Maybe because it would be quicker, or we don't trust the other person to do it properly, or maybe, because if they do a good job it might show us up.

All too often, we fall into the trap as managers, of taking on too much ourselves, solving our peoples' problems for them, instead of enabling them to do so themselves.

There's a great little book on this by Ken Blanchard from the 'One Minute Manager' series, called 'The One Minute Manager and the Monkey.' It goes something like this.

There we are at our desk and one of our team comes into the office. As they do so, look at the monkeys clambering on their back. It's easy to do this visually. We ask them what we can help them with and they tell us about this problem they have getting something done. All too often we simply offer to sort it for them, (which is maybe because it's quicker to do that... or we just are naturally helpful people) and at that point, watch the monkey jump from their shoulder onto yours. We deal with their other problems in the same way. Soon the team member leaves our office, monkey free, smiling and maybe skipping with relief. Our back is covered in monkeys! Sounds familiar? I always get nods of agreement when I describe this to people -they can see those monkeys!

There is a different way, which Mary practices. It's not that Mary is unhelpful - remember she believes her first role as a leader is to serve others - but serving others does not mean taking on their issues, it means enabling them to solve their own issues, so they leave you office with solutions, empowered, but with the monkeys still firmly on their backs!

Just a word on creative discipline as well. Mary understands that creativity is absolutely crucial. How can we move forward, as an individual, a team or an organisation, unless we can come up with creative ways of doing things, creative solutions? I am deeply concerned that we have lost that creativity in so many people and roles. We need to encourage it, to nurture it, to train and develop our people to be creative. If we are creative without being disciplined however, we stop focussing on our most important things, we become side tracked and we begin to hobby farm. The trick is to encourage, to champion creativity, but to ensure that it is delivered within a disciplined framework and in great teams and organisations that disciplined framework becomes part of the culture – 'what we do around here'. A powerful combination indeed.

Do seek to empower your people whenever you can. Take them out of their comfort zone into their stretch zone. It's in our stretch zones that we grow, develop, find new ways of doing things, become more effective leaders. Provide a sufficient level of support to prevent them drifting into their panic zones. I do think people spend far too much time in their comfort zones. There is a saying that we should all do one thing that scares us every day. I really do concur with this.

Empowering our people is crucial to ensuring they are engaged, but it is only part of the story. In his work on leadership in his book 'The 8th Habit', Stephen Covey argues that people give their best when they are fully engaged, that it is possible to engage our people at four levels; their body, heart, mind and spirit. There is too much depth here to go into full detail, and the book is well worth further examination, but each level can be summarised as follows:

When we engage someone's body we are at the entry level of engagement (there are close links here to Maslow's hierarchy of needs). We pay them a reasonable and fair wage for the job they are doing, we give them appropriate additional benefits to their employment, we give them the basic knowledge, skills and tools they need to do the job and we provide them with a safe working environment. Pretty basic needs, but we cannot hope to begin to engage our people unless these are in place.

We can do so much more, for we can also engage the heart. Now, we treat our people with respect, we praise them for a job well done whenever it is deserved (always being genuine) and we create a fun working environment, where coming to work becomes enjoyable.

Incidentally, a fun working environment can be created anywhere and is completely consistent with doing serious work. It's not about red noses and clown outfits, it's about having a laugh at work, working amongst friends, some social activity and can exist anywhere within any disciplined framework. I previously did some work for a high street bank. Their counter staff have a responsible job handling vast amounts of money. It's a serious business needing sensible, conscientious and diligent people. We succeeded nevertheless, in creating an environment where those people had fun at the same time.

So, we must engage our people's hearts, but we can do more - we can also engage their minds and this is what far too many organisations fail to do. It's such an easy win. When we engage the mind, we listen to our people, we want their ideas for improving things. We give them challenging assignments, we empower them, we want to give them more responsibility and unlock their potential. We want to give our people enhanced knowledge and skill, wherever appropriate we set out a career path for them. We want them to grow and flourish, just like those tomatoes.

Finally, the highest level of engagement is when we can engage someone's spirit. This is a little more difficult to explain, but when we achieve this we have engaged something deep inside the person. This begins to happen when people genuinely believe they are doing worthwhile work. They can see a link between what they are doing and delivery of the team's and organisation's vision and purpose. We have established that 'line of sight' we talked about in previous chapters. Leaders have painted a compelling picture of the future. Now, people believe they are doing important work. We work hard, to ensure there is a link between the values an individual holds dear and what a whole organisation stands for and demonstrates. Ultimately, we fully engage people when they feel they are contributing to a noble purpose.

It's become such a cliché, but remember the day Kennedy asked a janitor at Cape Canaveral what he was doing? The janitor's response, 'part of a team that is putting a man on the moon.' Here was one person whose spirit was engaged. Truly transformative leaders inspire deep commitment among many and have continued impact long after they have gone.

As Maya Angelou said:

'people will forget what you said, people will forget what you did, but people will never forget how you made them feel.'

There's so much to consider here, but hopefully this might interest you enough to want to learn more and also, like Mary, to think carefully about what you can do to engage your people at each of these four levels. Where trust is high, you can even introduce these four levels of engagement to your team, and discuss with them how engaged they are and what you could do to help build engagement.

One more thought - how engaged are you? Take a few moments to consider your level of engagement, of your body, heart, mind and spirit. Use your self-awareness to consider each dimension because if you are not highly engaged, it is far more difficult to engage your people.

As we build engagement we play our part in building a high performance culture. Culture is another of those buzzwords, simply defined as 'what it's like around here.' For me, a high performance culture is one that does engage people, which encourages and enables them to give their best every day, where people want to turn up and play their full part, where they feel empowered but supported, where creativity is encouraged, but alongside that creativity is a disciplined framework, responsibility and joint accountability. It's one where trust is at the heart. Maybe you can see so many of Mary's ten traits coming together in that description?

Once more we could cover many pages examining high performance cultures, but let me point you to two simple and powerful books for further reading, (no great academic tomes here!). One is 'Gung Ho!' by Ken Blanchard (again) and the other 'Fish!' by Stephen Lundin. Both tell great stories of amazing organisations.

I work with the Director of a major UK company who absolutely understands the importance of building a high performance culture. She has spent the last few years absolutely focussed on getting it right, within her function. She has created an environment where people genuinely enjoy coming to work, where great performance is recognised and celebrated, where poor behaviours are not tolerated, where there are clear, consistent communications and where innovation and creativity are championed within a disciplined framework. The step change in the effectiveness and performance of her function has been amazing.

There is just so much to go at here and I realise I can

only hope to scratch the surface. Mary deeply understands that to get the most out of her people, she must give them freedom - enable them to be creative. She also knows, however, she must balance this with clear frameworks and by encouraging a disciplined approach. Freedom always goes hand in hand with responsibility and accountability.

# Case Study

A few years ago I was involved in a major cultural change project, supporting the head of a large charity. He already ran a successful organisation, making a real difference to the lives of thousands of young people, an organisation that already employed many motivated and highly committed people supported by wonderful volunteers, but he recognised that if he could build a really special, high performance culture, even more would be possible.

Delivering cultural change is up there with the most challenging things any leader has to do. It takes time (I think it can take up to two years to deliver transformational change) and it is such a nebulous subject that it is tough to know where to start, how to communicate what needs to be done. The more tangible it can be made, the better.

So right up front, we decided on six areas of focus that we believed could bring about the required change. They were:

Building leadership capability throughout the organisation, with an emphasis on leadership through serving others.

Increasing levels of engagement, focussing on the four areas of body, heart, mind and spirit.

Unlocking the potential of people through developing a

culture of empowerment.

Encouraging people across the organisation to work more effectively together, within teams, but also between teams and departments and through this to build synergy.

Building a culture of discipline.

Creating a set of values, which would develop a behavioural framework for the whole organisation.

We then set up a series of workshops, putting together cohorts of people across the organisation, mixed by function but also, by hierarchical level. After introducing each of the six descriptions, we stepped back, giving people the space to explore each element, encouraging personal and joint responsibility and accountability, whilst providing support wherever necessary. Truly, 'freedom within a framework' in action.

These groups worked together to develop the values and behaviours framework, they explored leadership models together, identified barriers to cross functional working and solutions to those barriers, dug deep into their levels of engagement and came up with imaginative and creative ways of measuring progress.

Don't let me give you the impression this was easy. It took time, much effort, lots of soul searching, constant revisiting and prompting, but over time the magic began to take hold. Not only was there tangible evidence of progress, you could feel it as well.

It remains one of the most enjoyable and fulfilling assignments I have been lucky enough to be involved in.

## Self Reflection

How good are you at giving your people as much freedom as you can, within a clear and supportive framework? Think of a current example where you know you could give more freedom. How can you make this happen?

How would your people describe the current culture of your team or organisation? Ask them! Are the conditions you have created conducive with a high performance culture? What could you do to build that culture?

Do you sometimes find yourself with a back full of monkeys? How could you still be helpful, but ensure the monkeys stay on other people's backs?

## Further reading

Culture of Discipline chapter from 'Good to Great' by Jim Collins

'The 8th Habit' by Stephen R Covey

'The One Minute Manager Meets the Monkey' by Ken Blanchard

'Fish!' by Stephen Lundin

'Gung Ho!' by Ken Blanchard

# Notes

.

# Chapter TWELVE
## Joint Accountability

'Every excuse I
ever heard made
perfect sense
to the person
who made it'

Daniel T Drubin

Picture this scenario. You have allocated a task to one of your team. You have set out what you want them to do, and agreed deadlines. It's an important task, one that needs to be delivered in order to move forward. You step back and let your team member get on with it.

Soon, it becomes clear that progress is not being made. Deadlines are missed, reports go unwritten, deliverables you had been promised fail to materialise. What would you do? My guess is that you would intervene, summon the team member to your office, find out what is happening, hold them to account for their failure to deliver.

Now look at it from their point of view. You had outlined the task to them but they had not been clear on the outcomes required. Should they have sought clarity? Of course they should, but you seemed to be in such a hurry when you explained it, already checking your watch and preparing for the next meeting. There was confusion over deadlines, they thought you wanted the whole task completed before reporting in. Resource allocation was unclear, you had mentioned a budget but they had found it all a bit vague. They wanted to seek clarity, but you always seemed so busy, discouraging interruptions.

It couldn't happen with you and your team? Maybe not, but I see this scenario played out all the time in organisations. Mary knows it's an easy trap to fall into, but she tries really hard to avoid it. She does so because she believes deeply in the principle of joint accountability and tries hard to constantly apply the principle. It's the ninth trait she demonstrates as a highly effective leader.

She understands the absolutely essential need as a leader to hold her people accountable for delivering. As I have said before, there is nothing easy about working for Mary. Because Mary is such a pleasant and engaging person, this can sometimes be confused with being soft. There is nothing remotely soft about her. She always ensures that things get done, but always in the right way.

She therefore constantly holds her people to account. If she sets them a task with deadlines, she expects those deadlines to be met and the task to be completed. She never tolerates poor performance or poor behaviour. She addresses it, always fairly, always with empathy, but never ducking a difficult situation or conversation.

She also knows that is only one side of the coin. She cannot hold her people accountable without holding herself to account as well. When she gives her people a task, she ensures they understand exactly what is expected of them. She sets out and agrees a clear end in mind. She also takes time to scope the resources available to deliver the task. She ensures deadlines are clear and agreed. Only then, when she has checked for understanding, does she step back and give her people the freedom to deliver.

Mary never abandons them. As we explored in the last chapter, she gives them just the right amount of freedom but joint accountability means she is there to provide support throughout the process, striving to ensure it is at just the right level.

Mary also knows that you cannot hold people accountable, unless there are clear targets and measures in place. If there are no targets, how can anyone be accountable? If you set targets, you must also set measures. She understands the essential need to constantly measure how her teams are doing and establishes a whole series of measures at every level.

Mary understands the difference between lag measures and lead measures. A lag measure records something that has already happened. Sales last week, profit last month. They are important, but so many organisations seem to focus on these alone. Back in my corporate days, I lost count of the many hours I spent in meetings where the boss would be haranguing us over last month's sales. That's all very well - I loved watching them getting increasingly redder in the face, but it's gone - it's history.

Lead measures allow us to look at the likelihood of success in the future. The number of visits to prospect customers, the number of future orders secured, staff and customer satisfaction. Lead measures are essential because they look forward, not back. They are your prediction of future success, not your record of past results.

Mary understands that measuring customer satisfaction is a never-ending requirement. We all have customers, whether they are external or internal, and we need to constantly understand what they think of us, so we can strive to improve. Many organisations survey their customers, but often that is a cumbersome process, involving lengthy questionnaires, with a summary of results presented weeks later. It is so hard to take decisive action, certainly not real time action, with that approach.

Instead Mary uses the Net Promoter Score as a constant method of measuring her customer satisfaction. Designed by Fred Reichheld, 'The Ultimate Question' is so powerful because it asks just one question, which can be asked over and over again, can produce a measure that can be tracked over time and most importantly, includes a supplementary question that allows real time feedback to be acted on immediately.

The question asked is simply: 'how likely would you be to recommend (whatever product or service) to a friend?' Recipients score 0-10. The supplementary question then asks them why they have given that score. It's a very simple yet powerful question and formula, backed by loads of evidence-based research on the links between loyal customers and successful organisations. Get hold of the book 'The Ultimate Question' or search on-line. It's well worth a look.

Mary understands that she needs to know how her people are feeling, how satisfied they are. She does this at many levels, informally through listening to them, through taking time to do so at team meetings, through using the Net Promoter Score as a staff satisfaction measure and through more formal tools such as 360-degree appraisals.

*Mary holds herself accountable for constantly striving to improve as a leader but knows she cannot do it on her own. She recognises the value of coaching support and has also sought out a mentor.*

*A coach could be someone who provides support on a voluntary basis, individuals may be trained to provide coaching from within an organisation, but coaching is a profession that can be commissioned and paid for. Coaches are not there to provide all the answers but to give people the time, space, framework and challenge to find out the answers for themselves. Great coaches ask all the right questions and can help hold their clients accountable for agreed actions between sessions. It's very important to find a coach where the relationship really works for you.*

*A mentor fulfils a different role. They are usually more experienced than the person they are mentoring and understand at least enough about that person's role to be able to provide sage advice and help derive solutions. Mentors almost always offer their services on a voluntary basis, because they genuinely want to help. Seeking out the right mentor is again crucial, often it is someone you may have worked with at some point and really respect.*

*Mary has found that the support of both a coach and a mentor has been invaluable in holding her accountable and helping shape her leadership journey.*

*Joint accountability. It's a simple but crucial leadership trait, which we have dealt with in just a few paragraphs here. When it is consistently applied, as Mary strives to do, it can be a breakthrough point in getting consistently great results from your people. It takes time, it requires energy and it needs leaders who are relentless.*

# Case Study

You can't hold people accountable, you can't practice joint accountability, unless you know how you and they are performing. We have to put targets in place, supported by regular, robust and assiduous measurement. As they say, 'what gets measured gets done'.

I work with one company who use the Net Promoter Score consistently as their measurement of their customers' satisfaction. When properly applied, it is such a powerful tool. They are in the hospitality industry, running a chain of restaurants and hotels.

The drive to constantly measure customer satisfaction comes right from the top. If it didn't, there is no way it would be universally applied. The Chief Executive and his team recognise the crucial importance of regular customer feedback, and hold themselves accountable for ensuring it happens. They really do put the customer at the centre of everything they do. They recognise the central theme of Reichheld's work on the Ultimate Question - that customer loyalty is the absolute key to building sustainable profits.

On quite literally a daily basis, customers at their various businesses are asked the one simple question:

'How likely would you be to recommend this (restaurant or hotel) to a friend?'

Scores from 0-10 are diligently recorded.

There is then one simple supplementary question. 'Why?' Why have you given us this score today?

So simple to ask, taking less than a minute to complete, quick enough not to off put most customers.

The key then is not simply collecting the information, it's doing something with it. So, once a week (never less) the General Managers of these businesses sit down with their management teams. They note progress on their Net Promoter Score (tracking trends over time), but crucially they examine and act on the 'whys'.

'That staff member was rude'

'The food is too expensive'

'The toilets were dirty'

'The internet in my room was too slow'

'I received great service today'

'The quality of your food is excellent'

Simple feedback, which they can choose to deal with instantly, either by rectifying issues or ensuring praise is given where it is deserved. None of the above list is rocket science, but neither is so much about offering a consistently great customer experience If the sample of customers asked the question is also big enough, consistent patterns, common answers will occur.

Heads of Department are then held accountable for discussing the results and taking action within their own teams, who are jointly accountable for taking the necessary actions. Unit General Managers are held accountable for making sure it happens.

Back at head office, the senior team monitor, discuss and review scores on a monthly basis, ensuring their people have the resources and support they need to make the improvements. Joint accountability in action.

So does it work? Is all this effort worth it? Well, in just two years this company has raised its average NPS scores from the low twenties to consistently above seventy. Study Reichheld's work and you will know that gives sustainable competitive advantage. Sales and profits have consistently increased, as has staff satisfaction. Staff turnover is down, the right people are on the bus. Levels of engagement have never been higher.

Never underestimate the power of consistent customer satisfaction measurement and genuine joint accountability.

## Self reflection

Think of a time when you set a task for someone, with disappointing results. Consider it again in the context of the principle of joint accountability. Did you hold the person sufficiently accountable, did you deliver the necessary clarity, tools, freedom and support to give them the best chances of success? What would you do differently next time?

How satisfied are your customers (internal or external)? Do you really know? Do you consistently measure their satisfaction and act on the results? Could you use Net Promoter Score as a measurement and action tool?

How do you measure staff satisfaction in your team or organisation? Do you really know how satisfied they are? What are you doing to improve staff satisfaction?

## Further reading

'The Ultimate Question' by Fred Reichheld

# Notes

# Chapter THIRTEEN

## Relentlessness

'Surround yourself
with talent then
just grind it out'

Anon.

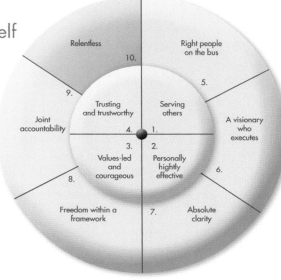

In this chapter we reach the end of our journey through
the ten traits that characterise Mary as a highly effective
leader. Her final trait is that she is relentless, she possesses
the determination and the ability to overcome obstacles
and set backs, to get back on course, to find a way
forward whatever the challenges she faces.

I love the quote attributed to Dale Carnegie:

'The important things in the world have been
accomplished by people who have kept on
trying when there seemed to be no hope at all.'

It's important to stress up front that there is no connection
between being relentless and being ruthless. Mary has

enormous determination, but she always strives to act and behave in the right way, in line with the values we examined earlier.

This is the final of Mary's characteristics, and I do not intend to make the case that any one characteristic is more important than another - they are all of equal importance in my view. Nevertheless, without the determination to succeed, the relentlessness to overcome obstacles, Mary would risk a high chance of frustration and failure in many of her endeavours.

It has been my privilege over the past few years to work with many leaders who possess this trait. The one I am going to tell you about is the Chief Executive of a large charity, and to a large extent, she has been my role model for many of the characteristics of Lead Like Mary that I have developed. She is an exceptional person. Remember though, you do not need to be at the head of an organisation in order to lead like Mary. You can be in any role, anywhere.

So, let me tell you this particular story. This leader joined her organisation as Chief Executive a few years ago. On paper, it was an attractive job, joining a charity that had an impressive history of doing great things. She was determined when she arrived to first take stock, not rush into making immediate changes. She shares my view that the first 100 days in a new job are crucial, a chance to look around you, to learn about the business and the people, to ask many, many questions and most importantly, to listen and not rush to judge.

She quickly discovered that although this was an organisation with a great past, it was currently struggling - things were in a poor state in many areas. This was not as good an organisation as the one she thought during the interview process. Perhaps she should have realised this, but remember, Mary is not perfect and she does not possess a crystal ball.

What this leader did, was learn very quickly during the first 100 days, through observing, listening, keeping an open mind and constantly questioning. She was willing to confront brutal facts. This is one of the traits of sustainably great organisations identified by Jim Collins and his team in 'Good to Great.' Unless we are willing to accept that there are brutal facts - things that just must be addressed and resolved before it is possible to move forward - we cannot make progress.

As Terry Leahy says:

'organisations are terrible at confronting the truth. It is so much easier to define your version of reality, and judge success or failure according to that. But my experience is that truth is crucial to both create and to sustain success.'

This leader wanted to build a great organisation, which is why she had taken the job. She was anxious to spend time with her people, developing a vision and strategy for the future, but she knew first there were things to resolve. I call this the 'fix it' phase.

So that is exactly what she did through much of her first year and beyond. Top of the list was putting the right people in place for the journey ahead, getting the right people on the bus (connections to other traits abound). This had to start with her senior team before she could move on. This was painful, there were good people here with many years of service, but some were never going to be equipped, in skills or attitude, for the next part of the journey. Making people-changes like this is never easy, it's not something Mary enjoys - these are real people with real lives - but Mary will always do the right thing in the right way, be firm but fair, never duck a people issue and this is exactly what this leader did.

Some of it was far from pleasant. It involved sleepless nights, and inevitably the prospect of legal ramifications. This leader was relentless, she knew that what she was doing was right and stuck at it, even through some fairly dark days.

There were also, of course, a couple of instances where difficult conversations resulted in people accepting that it was right for them to leave the bus. They recognised they were on the wrong bus and a dignified departure at the next stop would lead to a much more fulfilled life for them going forward.

The issues were not just restricted to people. She uncovered many things that had to be sorted urgently. Areas of unfinished work or poorly handled outcomes that were in danger of putting the whole organisation at risk, inadequate systems, broken processes. She met regular and energy sapping resistance, from people who did not want to accept change.

This is where Mary's characteristic of relentlessness really comes to the fore. Faced with such resistance, it would have been very easy to give up, either to seek a new job in greener pastures elsewhere, or to 'go native' and accept that she could not change things.

This leader did not do this - neither do so many amazing

leaders I work with - she knew what she was doing was right and even though she was often plagued by moments of self doubt, she had the inner strength to plough on, always questioning herself, never too single minded that she stopped doing the right thing, always determined to succeed with her eye on a future vision.

Over time, if you stick at it, and if you are consistent, if you can paint a compelling picture of a better future - things become a little easier, people begin to understand that you are serious, that you are here to stay, and that you are doing things in the right way. Respect begins to grow. Good people, who had previously felt held back, now come to the fore. They want to be part of the journey with you. They acknowledge and admire the fact that you do not duck difficult issues. Even previously resistant people begin to realise this might be a better way forward. Some people previously at the back of the bus, begin to edge forward.

For more than three years now, I have worked with and watched this leader as she has overcome obstacles, faced brutal facts, built the right team around her, set out a vision and strategy for the future and taken people with her through a myriad of small, consistent actions, day in and day out, never wavering in her determination. Much of her organisation is unrecognisable compared to the one she inherited. It's an object lesson in relentlessness.

We started this journey by exploring Mary's personal humility and lack of ego. We end it by focussing on her relentlessness. It's a neat circle because these are the two primary characteristics recognised in 'Good to Great' as Level 5 Leadership.

One other Jim Collins reference, which comes from his

new book, 'Great by Choice' further demonstrates relentlessness. In the '20 Mile March', Collins and his team found that organisations which had continued to thrive even in the most turbulent of times, had maintained steady progress over a number of years, they had not knee jerked back and forth, or delivered spectacular results one year followed by setbacks the next. They had continued to move steadily forward, day in and day out, year in and year out. They, to use his analogy, had crossed whole continents at twenty miles a day.

He likens it to Roald Amundsen's steady progress towards the South Pole in 1912, so focussed on small but steady progress, in contrast to Scott's chaotic and ultimately fatal mission. Powerful stuff.

We even return to John Kotter and his penguins to emphasise the point. The penultimate of his eight step change framework is 'don't let up, be relentless until the vision is a reality.'

It's well worth revisiting 'Good to Great' and reading the chapter called 'Confront the Brutal Facts'. Read the Stockdale paradox, an object lesson on overcoming seemingly overwhelming odds. Then read the chapter at the end of the book, 'The Flywheel and the Doom Loop'.

Mary possesses enormous levels of energy and resilience. When the going gets tough she confronts the brutal facts and finds a way through. Mary is relentless.

# Case Study

I wanted to finish the series of case studies with a personal one, which takes us away from the world of work. Remember, leadership is a whole life activity, it is not restricted to our paid employment.

Lots of leaders are involved in voluntary activities and assignments and for many of us it is up there with the most rewarding things we do. It can also often require us to be relentless.

I choose to serve as a trustee for a handful of charities, but the one that gives me the greatest pleasure is very close to home. I live in a small, rural community, a delightful village, Fradswell, familiar to those who read my weekly blog. Like so many other remote village, there are real issues to address, not least rural isolation, the lack of local employment opportunities, the distance to the nearest shop and other amenities and the lack of a bus service. This particularly affects more elderly people, but is also an issue for a younger generation who have no local facilities and often few reasons to want to stay, long term. We want to build and maintain a sustainable rural community that will be here for generations to come and therefore need to address these issues.

Our sole facility (besides one street light and one post box!) is an old, decrepit village hall. Over ninety years old it started out life as an army hut. It is now in a terrible state of repair, literally falling down.

Our challenge is to find the funds necessary to build a new village hall, not for the sake of having one, not so we can run the odd social night, but so we can deliver activities and services that will make a genuine difference to the community, including a community shop selling local food, activities for children, a weekly lunch club for the elderly, a place where we can enable people to meet, learn from each other and provide small enterprise opportunities.

The barriers to overcome have been enormous. We have been involved in a complex land swap, there is planning permission to obtain, numerous obstacles to be overcome and of course, we have to raise the funding, during very difficult economic times. We also have to keep the local community engaged, involve them, communicate regularly with them and carry out local fundraising.

All of this would be a challenge for an organisation with adequate resources. When you are in such a small community, relying on voluntary labour, usually given by already busy people and where apathy is the constant enemy, as is a resistance to change, the task becomes even more challenging.

That is when we need to be relentless; to overcome barriers, to confront brutal facts (not least failed funding applications), to try and create a sense of urgency, to paint a picture of the future, to communicate effectively. Day after day, week after week, year after year.

A small but committed and relentless group has been pursuing this project for five years now. There were many times when it would have been easier to give up, to accept it was not possible. We didn't and recently we received the amazing news that we have finally been successful in securing development funding for the project from the Big Lottery, only a few remaining hurdles now stand in the way of full funding to fulfill our dream.

This whole experience sits right up there with the things I am most proud of.

## Self reflection

What 'brutal facts' are currently preventing you, your team or organisation from being even more effective than you are already? Have you identified, discussed and faced up to these brutal facts? What can you do to help overcome them?

What is the single most frustrating thing about your job at the moment? Looking at the issue in a new light how could you approach it differently and overcome it?

Think ahead to a year today. What is the single most important change you want to have made by then? It could be to yourself, to someone else, with your team, at work. What can you do, from today, to give you the best chance of delivering that change?

## Further reading

'Great by Choice' by Jim Collins

'Our Iceberg is Melting' by John Kotter

The Confront the Brutal Facts chapter of 'Good to Great' by Jim Collins

# Notes

# Chapter FOURTEEN
## Becoming Mary

'It is not the strongest of the species that survive, nor the most intelligent, but the ones most adaptable to change'

Charles Darwin

'Whatever you can do or dream you can, begin it. Boldness has genius, power and magic in it'

Goethe

There you have it, the ten traits, which I believe, define Mary and make her a highly effective leader. I guess the inevitable question you may be asking at this point is 'so, what next?'

Well, here's my challenge to you. On the basis you have stuck with me to the end of the book I believe you already regard yourself as a leader and genuinely desire to be an even more effective one. There are countless leadership frameworks around, I am not suggesting that Mary's ten traits are any better than a host of other models, but I am convinced, after close on forty years of trying to be a leader and observing and working with many amazing leaders, they represent for me a pretty accurate picture of what great leadership is about. I want to encourage and enthuse you to resolve to become an even greater leader than you are already.

For to me, great leadership is the key to everything. It's what builds great companies, great charities, great schools, great hospitals and great institutions. It's what unlocks the potential of others. It's what makes a difference, builds a better world, every day, everywhere. It's what changes the world.

Organisations have become increasingly complex, which makes highly effective leadership even more challenging and essential. At one level however, leadership really is so simple. In 'Management in 10 Words' Terry Leahy recounts his reply when asked by the country's most senior civil servants how Tesco transformed from a struggling UK supermarket to the world's third largest retailer:

'Its quite simple. We focussed relentlessly on delivering for customers. We set ourselves some simple aims, some basic values to live by and we then created a process to achieve them, making sure everyone knew what they were responsible for'.

Clarity, values, accountability, relentlessness. It's all been there, as we've explored Mary's traits together. At one level leadership is so simple - but just because the principles are simple, it doesn't make them easy to apply. As Ray Noyes said:

'Anyone who says leadership is easy, hasn't understood.'

I already have the privilege of working with many 'Marys', leaders I admire and respect immensely, who are making that difference every day - already demonstrating the ten traits I have described. I also work with many people who aspire to become Mary, who truly wish to be great leaders. I come across them in all walks of life, in all sorts of organisations, at every level. The thing that binds them together, is their desire to do the right thing, to lead in the right way, to take people with them, to build that better world.

Organisations everywhere, society as a whole, is crying out for more effective leaders, people who are authentic, who really care, who want to deliver the right results but in the right way. In a way, I've written off many of the current generation of people at the top of organisations. There are exceptions, but many of them grew up in a world which was inhabited by too many 'Bills' and too many 'Sidneys'. I do think there is a chance to influence the next generation - those currently making their way up through organisations everywhere - who will take on bigger and bigger roles and will look at leadership in a different light.

I know I can only make a small contribution to that change. I established my own business a little over a decade ago with the purpose of:

'Inspiring and enabling leaders to transform the world of work by unlocking the potential that delivers amazing results.'

I can only try and influence a few people, but, deeply believing in the principle that leadership is an inside-out process, maybe those people will go on to teach and influence others. Remember the starfish story from earlier on? You being good enough to buy this book has made a small contribution to that process. What you decide to do as a leader, how you decide to make a difference, will determine what happens next.

You can join me in playing our small parts in this leadership evolution. Leadership lies at the heart of everything. Great leaders inspire those around them, unlock potential, build great organisations, deliver amazing results, improve communities, change society, ultimately change the world. We need authentic leaders at every level, who lead from the inside out and serve others. Leaders who lead like Mary.

I am so excited by some of the young, emerging leaders I am privileged to work with. I see such talent out there, so much potential. Let me tell you just about two of them.

The first is maybe thirty or so and has a middle level role in an environmental charity. He is absolutely committed to making a difference in the world and possesses enormous energy, vision, passion and determination. His particular interest is in conservation and he has set up a breeding programme for a previously endangered bird species. Not content with that, he has created links via the migration route of these birds, which now involve educational programmes bringing together children in the UK and Africa. He is the first to admit he is far from the finished article as a leader, several of Mary's traits would not currently be strong areas for him, but he wants to learn and improve constantly. His future ambition is to set up his own charity. One day, this leader just might change the world.

The second person is again in a middle ranking role, this time in the IT function of a major UK company. She is in her late twenties and I have had the pleasure of working with her for several years. When I first met her, she was just starting out in a junior role. It has been extraordinary watching her grow. She was determined from the beginning that she wanted to develop as a leader, but was the first to admit that she had so much to learn. She has very high self-awareness, constantly challenges herself, overcomes set backs, and combines real talent with absolute determination. She is already making a difference in a tough, commercial environment. I have no doubt she is destined for very senior roles and I also know that she will remain absolutely focussed on leading in the right way. She is, and will be, a great example of leading like Mary.

These two people are in very different roles. What unites them is their determination to become great leaders, their desire to lead in the right way and their willingness to learn.

Please remember that Mary is far from perfect. She is still learning every single day. She constantly challenges herself and is never satisfied. She always wants to improve. She has her fair share of self-doubt, she is desperate to do the right thing in the right way. She possesses real self-awareness and extraordinary determination. She just wants to make a difference to someone, somewhere every day.

Mary does so by being an authentic leader who truly believes her first role as a leader is to serve others. From deep within her character she strives to be personally effective, values-led, courageous, trusting and trustworthy. She strives to get the right people on the bus, to be both a visionary and someone who gets things done, to provide absolute clarity and freedom within a framework. She practices joint accountability and is relentless.

Mary is just a fictional character, but every day I come across real 'Marys' and want to be 'Marys'.
I would love you to join this amazing journey of discovery.

So, read this book, re-read it, write in it, dip into the further reading, take time out for the self reflection activities, visit the website, explore a variety of other leadership sources, find a mentor, keep the book as a reference point for the journey ahead, or pass it on to someone else.

Choose to go out there and lead like Mary. **Because you can.**

# So now what?

If this book has inspired you to learn more about Lead Like Mary and focus on your own leadership journey, there are many ways to stay in touch.

Visit the Lead Like Mary web site:

www.leadlikemary.com

where you will find additional resources and details of Lead Like Mary workshops and programmes

 Join the 'Lead Like Mary' group on Facebook

 Follow Mary on Twitter:  @leadlikemary

You can also keep in touch with Barry:

www.barrydore.com

 Follow on Twitter: @barrydore

E mail barry@barrydore.com

20212813R00111

Printed in Great Britain
by Amazon